MATCH OF MY LIFE

MATCH
OF MY LIFE

Twelve stars relive their greatest games

Liverpool

Leo Moynihan

This edition first published by Pitch Publishing 2012

Pitch Publishing
A2 Yeoman Gate
Yeoman Way
Durrington
BN13 3QZ
www.pitchpublishing.co.uk

A CIP catalogue record is available for this book
from the British Library

ISBN 978-1-9080516-7-7

Typesetting and origination by Pitch Publishing.

Printed in India by Replika Press Pvt. Ltd.

Acknowledgements

I'D LIKE TO thank my publisher Simon Lowe for approaching me to do the original hardback of this book and for all the patience, support and enthusiasm he has given the project. I'd also like to thank Paul Camillin of Pitch Publishing for taking on the publication of this paperback edition.

This book, of course, would not exist without the wonderful memories of all the players: the late Laurie Hughes, Ian St John, Tommy Smith, Phil Neal, Alan Kennedy, Mark Lawrenson, Jan Molby, John Barnes, Mark Wright, Gary McAllister, Jamie Carragher and a special mention for Ian Callaghan who helped get me in touch with some of the lads including Ronnie Moran. Thank you all so much for your time and for making a fan feel so comfortable and allowing me to shape your memories and words into these chapters.

I'd like to thank Ronnie Moran for his foreword, Steve Cook, Paul Dalglish, Steve Done and everyone at the Liverpool FC museum, Gary Double, Lawrence Hannah, Kira Milmo (Happy now!), Janet Ree, Kathryn Taylor at SFX, Steve Taylor for putting me up, Liverpool's taxi drivers for entertaining me and my late father John for his memories.

Leo Moynihan

Dedicated to the 96 Liverpool fans who lost their lives at Hillsborough on 15th April 1989

Contents

FOREWORD by Ronnie Moran 11

INTRODUCTION by Leo Moynihan.........................15

1. LAURIE HUGHES...19
Wolverhampton Wanderers 1 Liverpool 2
League Division One
Saturday 31 May 1947

2. IAN ST JOHN 39
Liverpool 5 Arsenal 0
League Division One
Saturday 18 April 1964

3. IAN CALLAGHAN 57
Liverpool 2 Leeds United 1
FA Cup final
Saturday 1 May 1965

4. TOMMY SMITH...73
Liverpool 3 Borussia Mönchengladbach 0
UEFA Cup final first leg
Thursday 10 May 1973

5. PHIL NEAL...91
Liverpool 3 Borussia Mönchengladbach 1
European Cup final
Wednesday 25 May 1977

6. ALAN KENNEDY 107
Liverpool 3 Tottenham Hotspur 1
League Cup final
Saturday 13 March 1982

7. MARK LAWRENSON 121
Liverpool 1 AS Roma 1
European Cup final
Wednesday 30 May 1984

8. JAN MOLBY...137
Liverpool 3 Everton 1
FA Cup final
Saturday 10 May 1986

9. JOHN BARNES...155
Liverpool 5 Nottingham Forest 0
League Division One
Wednesday 13 April 1988

10. MARK WRIGHT..173
Liverpool 2 Paris St Germain 0
Cup Winners' Cup semi final second leg
Wednesday 24 April 1997

11. GARY MCALLISTER 187
Liverpool 5 CD Alavés 4
UEFA Cup final
Wednesday 16 May 2001

12. JAMIE CARRAGHER..205
Liverpool 3 AC Milan 3
UEFA Champions' League final
Wednesday 25 May 2005

Foreword

by Ronnie Moran

I JOINED THIS wonderful club straight from school in 1949. I had been playing for Bootle boys and happened to know a postman who delivered letters to Liverpool's chairman. He kept recommending me until eventually I was asked to sign amateur forms. A week later I was playing my last game for Bootle when I was told there was a gentleman to see me. He was an Everton scout and he wanted me to sign for his club. 'You're a week late,' I told him and I'm glad he was.

I battled my way into the first team, making my debut at Derby in 1952, but I never knew just how much of an impact the place would have on me and my life. I left Liverpool Football club in 1998 and can only say that the 49 years I spent at the club meant everything to me.

There are so many occasions, so many great matches, so many great men and so many great players. To me, it was all started by one man though, Bill Shankly. When he arrived in December 1959, the club had settled for their place in the established order of things challenging for promotion from the old Division Two. I wasn't aware of it at the time as I was playing, but Shanks set about changing everything and that included instilling a winning attitude.

He was one of a kind. He would have excelled even more in the game today. He wasn't a bighead, but he loved being with and talking to the press. Today they have the big conferences and cameras everywhere after the match and Shanks would have lapped that up. Today's managers wouldn't have been able to keep up with him.

It was his giant personality that imposed itself on the place and created such a great club. The training was immediately improved as Shanks always felt that the work on the training ground should be enjoyable as that would be reflected on a Saturday. It was fun, but most importantly it was competitive.

Our five-a-sides were always keenly contested and Shanks was the worst, he hated losing and loved winning. I remember the night we won the UEFA Cup in 1973. Tommy Smith goes into detail in the book about that triumph, but what I remember is just how happy Shanks was with winning in Europe. The thing about him was he was equally ecstatic by beating the kids in a five-a-side at Melwood.

That was his attitude and it was passed on to players who shared the staff's desire not to lose. For 24 years I worked with the first team as a coach and I always tried to instil that craving to work hard and to hate defeat. I had to give out a few rollickings, mind. I remember having a right go at a young Jamie Redknapp. I was at him and at him to work harder because, as talented and skilful as he was, he was going nowhere without hard work. Jamie says today that that was the best thing that happened to his career.

Players today laugh at how much I shouted, but they understood and eventually they shared that desire for success. We, the staff, and the players were one of a kind. We all had our ideas and were encouraged to share them, but when it came to achieving our goals we were the same. That is why we won so many trophies.

I suppose some of the most memorable of these occasions were in Europe. I loved those nights. I actually played in the club's first game in Europe against Reykjavik at Anfield and so the first European Cup win in Rome in 1977 is a night I will never forget. Going back to Rome in 1984 was equally as impressive and joyous and that's why I took such pleasure watching the boys win a fifth European Cup in Istanbul.

I watched that game at Anfield amid 300 guests. At half-time there were a lot of heads down and even I, who spent years geeing the team up during the break, even I, who if there would have been shouting at the lads, "Come on you can do this," even I thought "This looks bad". Some fans came up to me saying we've got no chance and for some reason I took them up on that. "Hang on," I said, "this game has already thrown up the quickest goal in the competition's history, why not the best comeback as well?" It was and it was a great victory. One I believe only Liverpool Football Club could have pulled off.

The place evokes so many memories and even today the club is part of my life. I go to Melwood twice a week and have a walk with the players. When Roy Evans left I popped along and went to Gerard Houllier's office to ask if it was OK that I kept coming. Gerard stood up and said, "Ronnie, you are always welcome here, it is your spiritual home."

That has continued under Rafa, although I think he had to ask someone who I was, but when he found out, he made me very welcome. I still go to Anfield for every home game as the club gave me two season tickets. When I arrived for the first match after packing up I arrived at my seat and there was some interest from the surrounding fans.

The bloke in front of me turned and said, "You're not going to be sitting there are you Ronnie?"

"Yes, what's wrong with that?" I asked.

"Well, you're not going to stop shouting and hollering are you, like you used to do in the dug-out?" He was wrong, I don't do that anymore, I leave the shouting to others.

I hope you enjoy this book and that it takes you back to so many wonderful days and nights. My own personal favourite was a 4-0 win over Everton in the Cup in 1955. You never forget your playing days and to beat the old enemy like that was something special.

Introduction

THE TAXI PULLS up at the gates of Liverpool's training ground and there is a flurry of activity amongst hungry fans, their autograph books shaking expectantly as they hustle to get a look at the new arrival. They surround my cab and I'd be lying if I said I didn't feel a twang of misguided importance as the throng swelled. Two eager boys open the car door, notepads and pens at the ready, looking me up and down with hope in their hearts. "Who are you?" they ask.

"I'm the new Dutch centre-forward," I say hoping that my choice of nationality might excuse the slightly reddened eyes.

"No, he ain't!" shouts one slightly older and observant fan. "He's nobody."

With that their faces dropped and the relish that had greeted my arrival was replaced by a forlorn dejection as the car, unchallenged, chugged its way through the gates and toward the main building.

My kitbag housed only pens, paper and a Dictaphone, but how I wished it was keeping warm my size-elevens and a fresh jock-strap. At that point the disappointment on the faces of the young fans was matched only by the glum expression on my own.

As I paid the taxi driver I was racked by some unanswered questions from my youth. Why had I not been those few (OK many) yards quicker? Why had I not been blessed with a shot like Semtex or the agility of a gazelle in leg warmers? In short, the fact that I was not here as the new, lorded striker was causing me, a 32-year-old writer, as much angst as it had caused those young fans.

Now, having spent time with a dozen Liverpool legends, that want burns brighter. To be witness to their enthusiasm, to have noted how much their days in red meant to them and to have been lucky enough to sit and chat about some of the most memorable occasions in the club's rich history was a privilege.

I had arrived at Melwood to talk to Jamie Carragher. When I started the project Liverpool had just beaten the German side Bayer Leverkusen in the second round of the Champions League. They had played well, but wouldn't have had the big clubs around the continent sitting up all night worrying about the likes of Jerzy Dudek, Vladimir Smicer or Djimi Traore.

With each win and each plucky draw, Liverpool made their way to the final, by which time optimistic fans grabbed hold of any chink of light or lucky omen they could find. Take a comparison with the year of the club's third European Cup triumph 1981: In 2005 *Coronation Street*'s Ken and Deirdre had got married, as they had in 1981; Prince Charles had also got married, as he had in 1981; there was a new *Dr Who*, as there was in 1981.

Perhaps fans might have noted, as they made their pilgrimage to Istanbul that on that same night, 25th May, in 1965, against all predictions Mohammad Ali knocked out Sonny Liston in Maine for a second time. Forty years on and now it was Liverpool proving the doubters wrong. They bounced off the ropes of certain defeat and sent the mighty AC Milan crashing to the canvas. It was yet another unbelievable night in the club's long and remarkable history, and one that provides the perfect and dramatic finale to this book.

That afternoon, Jamie Carragher sat and talked with childlike glee about the most amazing night of his life. With every anecdote and with every nervous twitch (at times it was like he was replaying the game right there in the interview room) the cynical picture that we all have about the modern footballer was erased and replaced by genuine love of the game and the club that employed him.

Those memories of Turkey were only weeks old in Jamie's mind, but believe me, in decades to come he will be retelling these same stories with the same wild eagerness and with that same glint in his eye. Time can't tarnish the memories or dull the glories.

Laurie Hughes, a wonderfully chirpy Scouser, sat with me over a cup of tea in his home flicking through old photos of his playing days and describing the team-mates that had won Liverpool the title in 1947. Like Jamie, Laurie's enthusiasm for his time playing for Liverpool was contagious and I left his company with a fresh spring in my step.

Laurie and Jamie's are the book-ends to a selection of memories from men who helped make Liverpool FC a success right around the world. The list reads like a "Who's Who" of Anfield greats. Ian St John, Ian Callaghan, Tommy Smith, Phil Neal, Alan Kennedy,

Mark Lawrenson, Jan Molby, John Barnes, Mark Wright and Gary McAllister were all so accommodating and I can only thank them all for not only their time, but their zest for the subject matter.

Everyone has their favourite match, a game that when you close your eyes and concentrate, you are transported back to the terraces or the stand and the noise from the crowd fills your ears. I hope you enjoy this assortment of memoirs as much as I loved pulling them together and I'm sure you'll agree they are wonderful moments from a wonderful football club.

Leo Moynihan

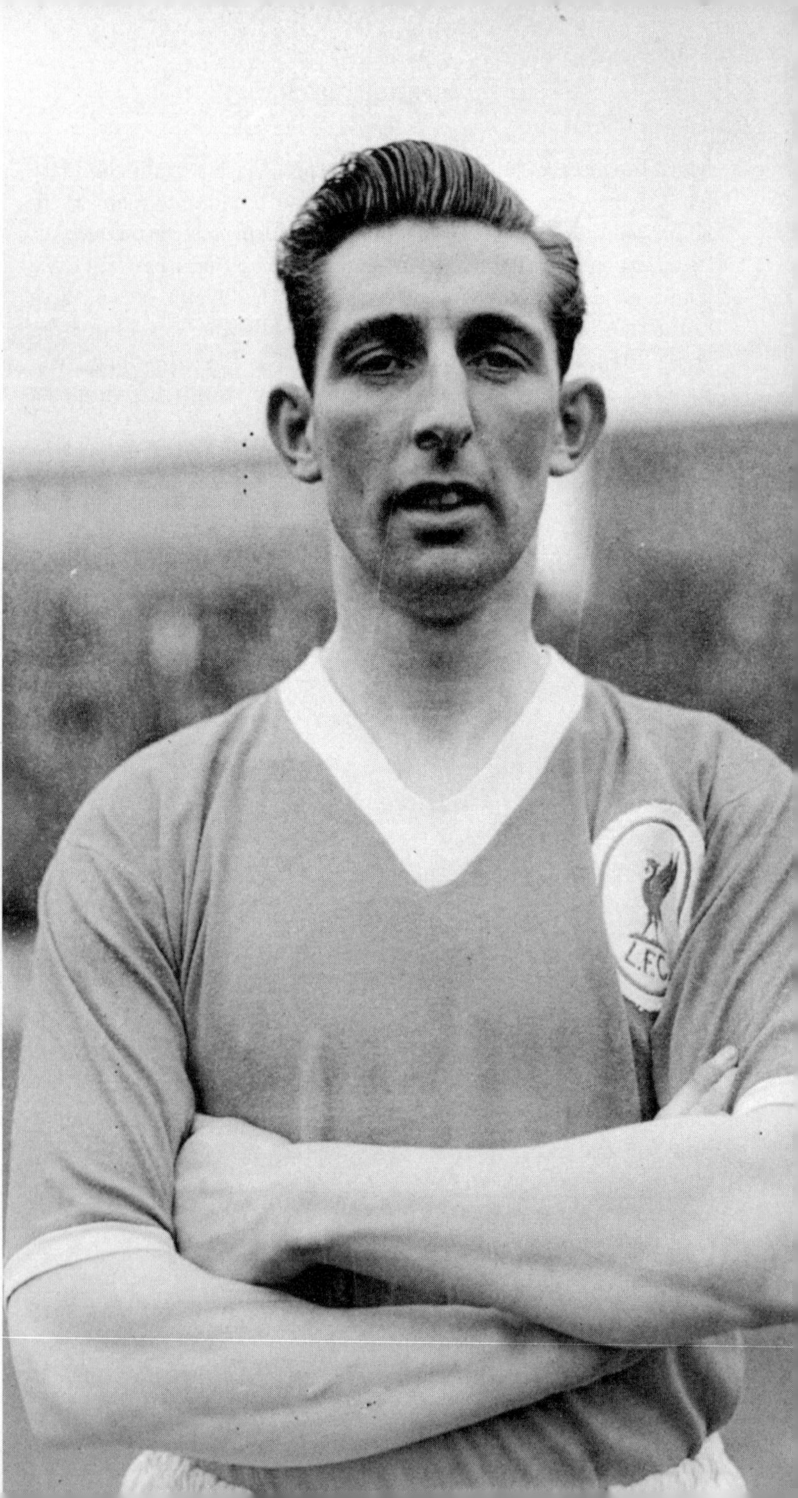

LAURIE HUGHES: BORN 2 MARCH 1924, LIVERPOOL; 326 GAMES, 1 GOAL

Laurie Hughes

Wolverhampton Wanderers 1 Liverpool 2

League Division One

Saturday 31 May 1947

FOR SO MANY Liverpool fans it must seem like such a long time ago. To the youngsters who go along to Anfield today it must seem like ancient history. Fading photos, the strange brylcreamed hair, the baggy shorts and sturdy looking boots. It's a world away from the glitz and glamour of the modern game, but when I look back at the photos of the Liverpool side that won the First Division Championship in 1947 it takes me rushing back to a wonderfully exciting time and it almost feels like yesterday.

It can be sad of course. Those guys in the photos were my pals, but today so many of them are no longer with us. What a bunch they were. They were top lads. We were very close and when the season came to the crunch it was that closeness and that collective will to win that saw us through and made us worthy champions. It was the last game at Wolverhampton Wanderers that stands out and underlined all of the qualities that took us to the title. We dealt with the pressure of the day and what had been a gruelling season, and we overcame tough opposition to achieve what we did. No one can take what we won away from us and that game at Molineux, along with that season, remains the most abiding memory of my 16 wonderful years at Anfield.

It was only Liverpool's fifth championship title, the club's first since 1922/23, but because it was the first season of top class football after six years of war, that victory at Wolves meant so much.

I had been only a young teenager when the war broke out and in many ways I was very fortunate. I got myself a trade and a job as a toolmaker and it was only towards the end of the hostilities that I got close to joining the services when I took exams for a flying crew. But soon the war was over and luckily I had missed it. The only action I saw was on the football field, as there were plenty of games to be played during those years and, when not working, I was in a football kit.

I GREW UP loving the game of football and during the war played for Tranmere Rovers. The Prenton Park club were keen for me to sign professional forms during my spell there, but I was earning decent money at work, so I declined. However, I decided that I should go pro when I reached 16, but perhaps not at Tranmere. My dad wrote to Everton and Liverpool Football Clubs in the hope that either would show an interest, but deep down he hoped it would be the team in blue who would snap me up.

My Mum and Dad owned a chip shop in Waverley near Sefton and every other Saturday would be the same. They would close the shop and go firstly to Goodison Park for the game and then off to the Empire for a night's entertainment. That was it. Without fail, that was their routine. Unfortunately for Mum and Dad, Everton wrote back and said I was a little too much on the small side for their club and so I had to wait tentatively to hear how the red half of Liverpool felt about my game.

It was a nervous wait. Despite my parents' allegiances, my brother and I both had soft spots for Liverpool and I guess you could say that, as our support for the Reds grew stronger, we had to disown our Blue parents.

I received word back from Liverpool, who said they were interested in looking at me. I had played against Liverpool on several occasions for Tranmere during the war. Despite the cancellation of the normal league programme and wartime travel restrictions, Rovers played games in the War League in the surrounding area. So I played against both the Merseyside clubs as well as the others in the north-west of England and you soon became aware of most players and their strengths or weaknesses.

I knew some of the lads at Anfield and played well for their reserves. The club liked what they saw and that good impression had me signing pro forms in 1943. I remember telling my dad I'd done well and that I was going to sign for the Reds. Let's just say there was a bit of tension in the Hughes household that day, but soon both my parents saw how much I wanted to be there and they begrudgingly became happy for me. The £10 signing-on fee that I received from the club seemed to help, as I didn't see a penny of it. I recall my dad's reasoning for having that off me was "I brought you into this world, son. You owe me!"

IN 1946, WITH the war over, the country yearned for top class football and nowhere was it more eagerly anticipated than in the city of Liverpool. The final season before the war began, 1938/39, had seen Everton crowned champions and so for six long years their fans had all the bragging rights in the town. Merseyside was such an upbeat place back then, despite the horrors of war. Being a major port meant that we had suffered terribly during the conflict, but gradually things were turning back to normal, and that meant regular football. The game meant so much and to have it back brought a spring to the city's step. It got everyone going. After all, what else was there? As the season approached I remember just how excited the public were at the prospect of First Division action. There was a real buzz about the place. For our part, we were all just so glad to be back doing what we loved best; playing football and playing competitively around the country.

The city had been devastated by the sustained bombing of the Germans and it would take years to build it up again, but in the meantime, us footballers could hopefully put a smile back on the faces of our fellow Liverpudlians. A day out at the football had always come with humour and a big part of a Saturday was centred on the laughter and the gags.

My favourite came a few years later when a young Alan A'Court, the club's centre-forward, was travelling from Prescot into a match at Anfield along with thousands of fans and was waiting to get the tram to the ground. On match days these trams would get jam-packed and, whilst all the lads squeezed on, Alan was left on the pavement. One of the wags from the docks saw who it was and shouted out, "Hey lads, you'd better make room for this one, he's bloody playing!"

THE MAN AT the helm was George Kay. Kay had arrived from Southampton to take over as manager of Liverpool in 1936. He already had a giant reputation in the game following a successful playing career that saw him captain West Ham United in the famous "White Horse" FA Cup Final of 1923. That game was to have quite a bearing on the history of Liverpool Football Club. Not only did Kay arrive at Anfield, but his opposing captain that day at the new Wembley stadium was Bolton's Jimmy Seddon, who joined Kay at Anfield as the first team trainer. George had inherited a group of players that were some way behind their rivals across the Park and the 1930s saw Everton by far the more dominant team on Merseyside.

George, though, was constantly thinking about how to improve and focused on nothing else other than the game, his players and success. To me, George was quite a dour man. I was one of the jokers in the team. I liked to play and train with a smile on my face, but George frowned upon too much fun so we didn't always see eye to eye. He was so desperate to achieve things that he often forgot to have fun and I found that side of his character hard to relate to. You had to respect him though. He knew what he wanted, he was football mad and that ultimately helped the team to succeed.

As well as Kay, Liverpool had a new chairman. Billy McConnell had taken the position in 1944 having made a lot of money in the local catering industry. He was a wonderful and generous man and, because of his work, we could go and eat anywhere in the city. In fact, we ate like kings as McConnell also ensured that plenty of food - real luxury in post-war rationed Britain - was sent to our training ground at Melwood.

It seemed food and what we ate had a big part to play in the Liverpool way back then. So much so, that it helped dictate exactly where the club went on our pre-season tour. George loved the United States and took us out there in the summer of 1946 positive that the juicy steaks served in America as well as their fresh orange juice would be the perfect preparation to the new season. He thought that the more we tucked into the better we'd do and looking back maybe he had a point.

We took the boat and were forced to do our running around the deck for the three days of the voyage across the Atlantic. I suppose being footballers we could have got bored on that journey, but it proved a very enjoyable trip. The *Queen Mary* normally sailed from Southampton, but had retained most of the crew who worked on her when she'd sailed from Liverpool on wartime service carrying troops and supplies across the Atlantic. Basically the ship was crammed full of Scousers and we would spend the time laughing, socialising and playing deck-tennis.

In New York we stayed in Brooklyn before travelling to Chicago and Canada, playing several games in what proved such an exciting tour. Some of us had never been abroad before and the whole experience was so new and so incredible. I loved it and it seemed the people loved us.

We got some massive crowds and wherever Liverpool went there was a huge interest in us and in the game. Four years later I would get a close look at the American game when they embarrassingly beat England in the World Cup of 1950, but for now I could do nothing but enjoy the country and its people.

One evening I went into an all-night diner and filled my plate to the brim before going to pay at the till. The guy working there noticed my accent and said, "Hey you're a limey." I told him I was a footballer from Liverpool and his face lit up. During the war he had been stationed in Warrington and had fallen in love with the area. I got a free meal that night and it just goes to show that us Liverpudlians were loved worldwide years before those Beatles boys had anything to do with it.

We returned from the United States feeling good and confident about the season that lay ahead. Why not? We had a great spirit (helped by our trip), a workaholic manager and, most importantly, some very good players. Liverpool had kept many of its key pre-war stars, but had sadly lost the great Matt Busby, who'd been club captain and something of a legend in the pre-war years. Busby had been offered a coaching role at Anfield, but instead opted to take over as manager at Manchester United. No matter, ours was a squad good enough, we hoped, to challenge the best of them.

In Cyril Sidlow, who'd signed from Wolves in February 1946 for £4,000, we had a very experienced and dependable goalkeeper. Thirty-year-old Cyril became a full Welsh cap after appearing in wartime internationals. In fact in one so-called Victory international at the Hawthorns in 1945, Cyril had played in goal for Wales while his clubmate Bert Williams, who'd ousted Cyril from the Wolves first team, played for England. Cyril was coming to the end of his career and arrived at Anfield after Wolves manager Ted Vizard opted to select 24-year-old Williams as first choice. Cyril was determined to prove that the Wanderers were wrong to let him go. Cyril wasn't what you would call an agile keeper and his concentration could wander, but his distribution to feet was excellent and he had very solid hands and was extremely confident.

In defence we had wonderful strength in depth. Jimmy Harley was a fine right-back from Scotland. He was a fantastic runner and had won many sprint races in his native country. The thing about Jimmy was his toughness. He didn't stand for any nonsense, not Jimmy. He was a typical hard Scotsman, a real tough nut and no one ever got past him. If they did, they were sent right over the Anfield wall. He'd managed to get himself sent off in the last league game before the war. Thankfully the FA didn't carry his suspension over to the 1946/47 season!

We also had Bill Jones, who didn't play enough games that season as he was late leaving the army. His grandson, Rob, later played for the club as a right-back in the 1990s and even followed his old granddad by winning England caps too. Eddie Spicer was a great, strong defender, whilst Ray Lambert was so important to the defensive unit. He was typically Welsh. On the pitch he was hard as nails, but off the pitch he was a very mild, charming and likeable character. He had actually signed for Liverpool as a 13-year-old back in 1936, but because of the war didn't get a chance to make his League debut until August 1946, ten years after signing!

None, though, were more likable than Bob Paisley. Bob played alongside me in defence, at wing-half or at left full-back. He was a no-nonsense player. There was nothing spectacular about Bob, he would often simply make a tackle and knock the ball to myself or Bill Jones to start an attack. That was Bob, quiet and reserved.

He wasn't much of a talker either. He wasn't one to sit and yarn about the ins and outs of the game; in fact he often quite amusingly struggled for any words at all. Unbeknown to us all though, Bob was taking everything in, noting the simple aspects of the game which he would use in years to come as the most successful manager the club has ever seen. Good old Bob.

Up front we were also strong, but before the season started George Kay felt we were perhaps lacking a goalscorer. Our captain, Jack Balmer, was a very good player and had been around for many years. He had a great goalscoring record, but he couldn't be expected to do it on his own. Jack wasn't the type of player who would battle alone up front and take the harsh treatment that could be dished out by the country's defenders. He didn't like the rough and tumble aspect of the game. Jack thrived on running on to balls and his speed often saw him race clear of those nasty centre-halves and that's how he got so many of his goals.

Having said that, any striker would get his fair share of chances with the likes of Billy Liddell around. Billy was the team's match-winner. He had everything and became adored by our legion of fans who soon nicknamed him simply "King Liddell" and the club itself "Liddellpool". George Kay had done well in signing Billy in 1939, promising the young Scot's parents that he could continue his accountancy exams. Despite being an outstanding outside-left, Billy could play anywhere in the forward line, but his main asset was his strength - both of stature and of shot.

My God, he was strong, but make no mistake; he was strong, but not dirty. Billy was a real gentleman, but once on the ball, there was no way you could shake him off of it. He was a powerhouse, lithe and sinewy, and the most perfect striker of the ball. He could hit it all right and you had to feel sorry for any silly defender who daftly managed to block one of his shots.

THE STRANGE THING was that players such as Bill Jones, Bob Paisley and Billy Liddell, who had all been at the club for a number of years, wouldn't make their full debuts until the 1946/47 season kicked off on 31st August. It was to be my debut too and the opposition were Sheffield United. We won the game

1-0 at Bramall Lane, but had to wait until the last minute before a little known player, Len Carney, in one of just six first team appearances he made for the club, scored what would - in the season's grand scheme of things - prove a vital goal. Len had won a Military Cross during the war, but didn't talk about the action he'd seen or why he'd been awarded such an honour. It wasn't the done thing, especially when so many had perished. You just got on with things - and anyway we were back playing football now. Better times were ahead.

We then lost 0-1 at Middlesbrough before taking on Chelsea at Anfield. That game saw Bob Paisley make his first team debut and what a game to start with. I had the dubious pleasure of marking Tommy Lawton that day, who had joined the London club from Everton at the end of the war. Tommy had been a hero at Goodison Park and my parents had idolised him, so it was good to pit my wits against a player, who in terms of centre-forwards, many regarded as the best.

Nearly 50,000 were packed into Anfield for the first league game since the war. The atmosphere was electric and by half-time they had cheered us to a 4-0 lead against a decent Chelsea side and after 50 minutes we were six up! Bill Jones was playing in the number nine shirt that day, which was testimony to his versatility. He scored a couple, whilst Liddell was running the Londoners ragged. Or so we thought. Chelsea suddenly got their game together and pulled the score back to 6-4. The crowd were stunned and it took a late Balmer goal to seal the game. It was an incredible match and, if the crowd had waited patiently for so long for their beloved football, then that match more than made up for lost time.

Our next game was also a goal-fest, but this time all five efforts went to Matt Busby's Manchester United as they took us apart at Old Trafford. That defeat provoked Liverpool's board to take a bold step into the transfer market and that proven goalscorer that I mentioned we needed was snapped up. His name was Albert Stubbins.

Albert had been scoring a lot of goals throughout the war at Newcastle United and had attracted a number of clubs. He seemed destined to move to Everton before our chairman, Mr McConnell, took matters into his own hands and travelled to St James' Park one Wednesday night knowing full well that Everton's officials were busy with a midweek game at Goodison. Mr McConnell offered a club record £12,500 for Albert; in fact he became the second most expensive player in history after Bryn Jones, who'd moved from Wolves to Arsenal before the war for £14,000. Newcastle could hardly refuse that amount of cash. I recall Albert telling me that he had been sitting enjoying a film in a local cinema when suddenly the show was interrupted with the words on the screen, "Will Albert Stubbins immediately report to St James' Park." The deal was done and Everton were furious.

It was a masterstroke. Not only had we outfoxed our arch rivals, we had signed a player who would complete a fantastic forward line and help us challenge for and ultimately win the title. Albert, like Billy, was a match-winner, and, unlike Jack Balmer, he loved the rough stuff. He actually thrived on the treatment given to him by defenders. I used to note how much he loved rubbing up against the enemy. If a defender was going to try and intimidate Albert he was going to have his work cut out. Our Albert was always up for the challenge and would simply use his shoulders to see off the challenge, all the while keeping complete control of the ball. That takes some doing.

Nat Lofthouse of Bolton had the same sort of strength. He was a colossal player and, try as I might, I could never knock big Nat off the ball. It unsettles defenders when forwards are not intimidated by the physical side of the game and instead actually thrive on it. I watch this boy Wayne Rooney today and he is the same. He would have done well in my era, as he likes to mix it with the opposition. You can see him enjoying that side of things and that, I'm sure, makes him so hard to play against.

Strangely and brilliantly, Stubbins' arrival at the club really galvanised Jack Balmer into action. He had always been a good player, but with Albert sharing the load alongside him up front, he became much more confident and in November he incredibly scored three consecutive hat-tricks in wins over Portsmouth, Derby and Arsenal. And he went on to score in seven consecutive games. Jack was the first man ever to score three league hat-tricks on the spin and it's a feat that's not been equalled since. His goals were invaluable as we had been very inconsistent and would be right up to the latter stages of the campaign.

IN EARLY DECEMBER we faced Wolves at Anfield. Wolves were one of the strongest sides in the country and boasted the talents of Stan Cullis, their legendary centre-half and a young Billy Wright who would go on and win over 100 caps for England. Their presence meant a huge crowd at Anfield. The official figure was a capacity 52,512, but if you ask me there was more than that packed in that day. Fans would always find a way of getting in by hook or by crook and it felt and sounded more like 65,000 crammed onto every inch of the terraces.

Anfield was such an amazing place to play football. It was the closest thing I've had to a spiritual feeling, it really was. The Kop was always heaving, but there weren't the songs that we have today. Songs such as You'll Never Walk Alone came much later, but back then you would just hear fans shouting, whistling and often joking.

They could be so funny and it was the Boys' Pen that always had me in stitches. I remember we had a young lad in our reserves. His Dad was our trainer, Jimmy Seddon, and this lad was quite unfortunate looking. By that I mean he was a gangly youngster, a little awkward let's say. The reserves were playing at Anfield in front of a big crowd (I told you we love our football in Liverpool) and this kid was sprinting down the touchline after the ball when one wag shouted out "Somebody open the gate!" Even I laughed and I was playing.

Unfortunately there was nothing to smile about the day Wolves came to Anfield as we were hammered 5-1. I remember Dennis Westcott scored four against us, which was hard to handle because he was an ex-Evertonian. They also had a good winger called Jimmy Dunn, who had played alongside me in schoolboy football.

Whilst we were stuttering in our challenge for the title, football itself was in dreamland. Almost a million fans had turned up at matches around the country on the opening day of post-war football and many clubs were experiencing consistent crowds of 50,000-plus.

It wasn't rare for the gates at Anfield to be closed over an hour before kick-off and that clearly highlighted just how popular the game and us players had become. What didn't follow that boom in the game was the players' wages and well into the season there was a real threat of industrial action by the players.

That threat was quite right too. We earned too little. I was on less than £10 a week and we campaigned for £12 per week during the season dropping to £10 in the summer months. Our demands were eventually met in October, but looking back it still wasn't enough. We were bringing record amounts of people into the grounds of England, but the most I ever earned was £14 a week. Something was wrong. Players today earn more in one match than I did in over 20 years playing the game.

Whilst the lack of cash in our wallets threatened to disrupt the season, it was the snow and the ice on the pitches that did exactly that. The winter of 1947 was terrible. Record snowfall and unimaginable low temperatures saw the much-awaited season dogged by postponed matches, but in a way it seemed to help us as, once the season was up and running again, we became more and more consistent and put together a run that gave us half a chance of taking the title.

I HAD MISSED a big chunk of those winter months after I fractured my leg in a home game against Bolton in January. I don't recall how it happened now. All I remember was lying on the side of the pitch in some considerable pain. Fortunately I was a strong bugger and I returned for the run-in just as the winter thawed and we began to play games again. I would love to say that it was my presence that changed our fortunes, but I doubt many people would believe it. No one believed that we had a realistic chance of the title that was for sure. Of our last eight games, five of them were away from Anfield and too many - even the fans - it seemed the best we could hope for was a commendable runners-up spot.

The season stretched out into the summer months as restrictions still enforced by the government meant we could only play on a Saturday, supposedly so the attraction of midweek football didn't interrupt the important business of working to rebuild the country. Remember, there were no floodlights then so all midweek matches would have had to be played in the afternoon. And I think plenty of fans would have ducked out of work for the afternoon to watch the exciting football that we were serving up, especially as we were still very much in with a shout of the title.

Stoke City, Wolves and Manchester United were all in the running and we did a lot for our cause when we beat United on 3rd May at Anfield thanks to an Albert Stubbins strike. We then had three games in London which saw us draw with already relegated Brentford, but beat Charlton and Arsenal. Even though we slipped up against the Bees, the other contenders had also been dropping points left, right and centre. United drew at Preston, while Stoke ended an unbelievable run of seven consecutive wins by drawing at home to Sunderland. Then Wolves lost at home to Everton. It's not often the blue half of Merseyside does the red half a favour, but they did that day. Going into our last game at Wolves, it wasn't in our hands, but we knew we had to beat the Midlanders to stand any chance at all of winning the title.

Manchester United had finished their campaign with 56 points. Wolves too were on 56 points whilst Stoke, like ourselves were on 55 and also had one game remaining. We were confident. Our form was great and it seemed that we were the team peaking at the right time. Mr Kay had us all very well drilled. We knew our roles and each player knew exactly what he had to do. We also had a squad full of players who could fill in for an injured team-mate without much fuss. That meant, that even when key players were missing, the team continued to play well with their more-than-able replacements.

Wolves, though, were clear favourites to win the game, and in many experts' eyes, were favourites to take the title. They had a fine team - they would go on to win the FA Cup and the League Championship in the coming seasons - they had beaten us easily at Anfield only months before and they had a fanatical support crammed into Molineux; a hard place to go and play at the best of times.

THE CROWD OF over 50,000 were always going to make life hard for us and produce a lot of noise, but they got even louder and passionate when they heard the news that their idol and captain Stan Cullis had announced that this would be his last game for the club. Their hero was retiring and it was time to give him a glorious send-off.

The fans weren't the only ones. Wolves' players said later they were desperate to win for Stan and so we faced an even more hyped up team and set of supporters. We had no idea before the game of Stan's decision to quit. Stan was well liked by us pros and had been born on Merseyside, but in the dressing room the first we heard of his retirement was when a roar went up as the news was announced over the loudspeakers and it slowly filtered through to us.

Things like that didn't bother us. Not even Cyril Sidlow, who'd been a team-mate of Stan's throughout the war. We were focused on what we had to do and in fact all the talk about Stan and the desperation with which Wolves wanted to win probably helped us and hindered them. George Kay sent us out simply stating that we should carry on doing what we had been doing, not to worry about the occasion or what was at stake and to give our small band of travelling fans something to shout about.

We would be missing Bob Paisley and Willie Fagan who were both injured. Eddie Spicer, normally a full-back, deputised for Bob, while, to replace Willie, Billy Liddell was moved to inside-left for the first time with the South-African winger Bob Priday put in at outside-left. As I said, things like that rarely disrupted the team's rhythm; Billy Liddell wasn't the type to let a new position worry him.

I remember running out of the dressing room and being hit, not by the noise, but by the heat. It was bloody boiling. Liverpool's local paper, the *Echo*, thought the ground looked more like Melbourne's Cricket Ground with the fans wearing shirtsleeves. It was the last day of May and here we were playing a match that was supposed to be played in mid-April. I recall the sight of a sea of handkerchiefs tied at the corners over the fans' heads to shield away the sun. It must have been 90 degrees that day, but as the game got going it seemed much, much hotter.

The St. John Ambulance men were very busy that day having to help the fans who were fainting in the heat. I suppose it added to the tension of the afternoon as, throughout the game, fans were being carried out from the stands and given medical attention. The officials too had to take steps, as the black they usually wore would have been too hot. Instead, they wore white cricket shirts that kept them that bit cooler.

Because of our great form – we had won six and drawn one of our last seven games – we started confidently and, with Billy Liddell in top form, it immediately felt like it could be our day. Wolves had more of the ball, but I felt we were comfortable. Their forward Jimmy Mullen shot just wide with a half chance and Harley attempted an elaborate overhead kick that flew over, but they weren't clear-cut chances.

Wolves had the crowd roaring them on, but you could sense that maybe their fans would begin to get a little frustrated as Mullen muffed another chance and Liddell began to run at their defence. Billy Wright pulled off a wonderful last-ditch tackle on Liddell early on and we knew if we could keep our Billy on the ball then they would have a lot to think about.

Despite the weather, the game was played at a fast pace. There was everything at stake and neither team wanted to sit back, so we both went for it. No wonder the crowd were fainting. We felt strong in defence though. I was pleased with how I was playing and I managed to make a number of good blocks and tackles to thwart their attackers.

I felt even better after 20 minutes when Jack Balmer scored to silence the raucous fans with his 24th goal of the season. He played a lovely one-two with Billy Watkinson that really split the Wolves defence in half before slipping the ball past Bert Williams.

You could tell that Wolves were totally hyped up and, after they'd gone a goal down, they really started to push forward. Alf Crook, Mullen and Jesse Pye all had efforts on goal, but Cyril Sidlow was on top form that day. He was blocking and catching everything. He was desperate to show his former manager, Ted Vizard, that he should have kept him on. Nice one, Cyril!

Wolves pushing on suited us. Albert Stubbins fancied his chances against the ageing Cullis and, before the game, had pulled our young winger Bob Priday to one side and suggested he simply loft some balls up and over the defence for Albert to run on to and test the departing Cullis' pace.

That's how we scored our second. Wolves had won a corner, which we defended comfortably and the ball fell to Priday in his own half. Bob looked about and, remembering what Albert had advised him before the game, he stroked the ball forward and sent Albert on his bike. Albert had a yard on Stan, but also had the great Billy Wright in pursuit. Our striker was going to get to the ball first and I remember noting that Cullis was huffing and puffing and had no chance of catching him. I really thought the centre-half was going to pull Albert back but he didn't and, as Albert advanced on goal, he coolly slipped the ball into the net.

Later a lot was made of whether Stan should have simply held Albert back. He wouldn't have been sent off in those days and many of his own fans wished he had done the ungentlemanly thing. Stan said that he didn't want to be known as the player whose professional foul had a hand in the Championship race, which is all very nice, but I think it's a lot of nonsense. Albert was simply out of reach and had shown Cullis a clean set of heels. There was no way he could have fouled him, even if he had wanted to.

Looking back on it, it was a classic goal. We took all their pressure and hit them on the break. You hear about all the great teams today doing that. Chelsea, Manchester United and even Liverpool play on the break and that's what we did in 1947. Before half-time they continued to push for a goal, but could only manage another shot from Pye that again flew high over the bar. I remember hearing one of the home fans shouting desperately, "It's not rugby, Jesse!" That made me laugh.

WE TRUDGED INTO the dressing room having shut the crowd up and knowing we were well worth our two-goal lead. Our manager was pleased, but as ever wouldn't let the occasion get to him or to us. He sent us out for the second half expecting a lot of pressure and he was right. Wolves really got at us and we could easily have wilted in the heat, but we kept our shape and our belief. I was very busy though.

I was enjoying the match. I had plenty to do and felt I was doing it well and was also very confident about Sidlow behind me. The ex-Wolves goalie continued to stop their shots and we continued to look dangerous on the attack. In fact, we had a Billy Liddell goal disallowed for offside and Stubbins really should have scored after good stuff from Balmer. Albert, and this was rare, rushed his chance and with only Williams to beat hit it straight and softly at him.

With 25 minutes left, Jimmy Dunn scored a good goal. Eddie Spicer made a hash of his clearance, but Jimmy still had a lot to do and coolly lobbed Sidlow in our goal. We still had plenty to do to defend our lead, but I wasn't one to get nervous and panic. None of us were, I don't think. I was more worried about my leg, which was becoming very sore. I suppose having fractured it, less than six months before that was to be expected, but there were no subs then and I wasn't going to leave us with ten men was I? I limped about doing what I could. Even Billy Liddell mucked in and moved back into defence to thwart Wolves' aerial threat. We had to dig in, but to be honest we didn't allow them a clear-cut chance and never felt really uncomfortable.

I myself was, mind. My leg got worse and I had to move to outside-left for a while. I'd like to say that I played like Stanley Matthews out there, but I'm no winger. After a while my leg loosened up a bit and I made my way back to the centre of defence.

I never felt we were going to throw it away as we had such a good mental strength. That was perhaps even more important to us than our footballing ability. We could be very hard to break down and that was down to our strength in character and after a lot of hard work we got the two points in what were very hard and very hot conditions.

It was a strange atmosphere at the final whistle. The Wolves' fans and their players were very upset and they also had the emotion of saying farewell to the departing Stan Cullis. On the other hand we were pleased to have won, but we couldn't celebrate as such as we had to wait for two agonising weeks until Stoke played their last game at Sheffield United. If they won they would be champions on goal difference, simple. Stoke had a good side, but had lost the great Stanley Matthews only weeks before the end of the season.

He'd been mysteriously sold by manager Bob McGrory after a long-running feud between the pair despite the fact that City still had this game left to win their first-ever trophy. Losing Matthews would have been a blow to any team and we were delighted that they'd sold him to Blackpool. Still, City must have fancied their chances and all we could do was wait. That was far worse than anything Wolves had thrown at us at Molineux.

THE DAY FINALLY came around and, whilst Stoke were playing at Bramall Lane, we were entertaining Everton in the Lancashire Senior Cup Final. The weather had been particularly bad in Yorkshire and so most of United's home games had been postponed between January and March. The fixtures were redrawn and Stoke had to wait until 14th June to play their last game at Bramall Lane. We were confident. The Blades were good. They'd actually won the 1945/46 league title, although that was still played under the wartime restrictions of movement and player availability so didn't count as a full League season. They'd also beaten both Stoke and ourselves on our own grounds, so we knew that City would not have it easy.

I think most of the 40,000 crowd at Anfield that day were listening for news from Yorkshire rather than watching us play. There were loud cheers in the ground as goals were announced. Sheffield led early on, but then Stoke pegged them back. The cheer was even louder when the Blades went ahead again early in the second half. We knew what was going on over the Pennines, but we still had to concentrate as we had a Merseyside derby to win. We were still playing; I think there was about five minutes to go when the final score from Bramall Lane came over the tannoy. Our chairman Bill McConnell announced it: Sheffield United 2, Stoke City 1. We'd done it. There was a huge roar, one that would have rivalled Hampden Park and hats were thrown into the air by the thousands of fans packed into Anfield. Both teams stopped playing and we were rewarded with a handshake from our Evertonian opponents before celebrating in the centre-circle with a happy huddle. We carried on playing, mind. And we had some defending to do, but managed to focus enough to hold on to win the game 2-1. I suppose these days you'd call that a double whammy!

It was a strange feeling. I wouldn't say it was an anti-climax, we were champions of England and it was great, but the two-week wait had, ever so slightly, taken the edge off what we'd done. We had won the league, but I felt that was just a matter of course. I felt that we *should* win the league and now we had. That was that. It's only later when you look back at your achievements that you feel ever so proud.

And I feel proud to have been part of a great team and an even greater set of blokes. I look at football today and I think I would have been able to hold my own. The money would have been nice, but I wouldn't change my team-mates for the world. They were a smashing bunch and, to me, my years at Liverpool Football Club were the greatest of my life. It was an education and made me a far better person than I may have been. I got to travel the world and see things I would never have seen and, thanks to that win in Wolverhampton, I can say I was a champion of England.

The memories fade a little, but the joy remains. I loved every minute of it, but then again who wouldn't? It wasn't like a normal job was it?

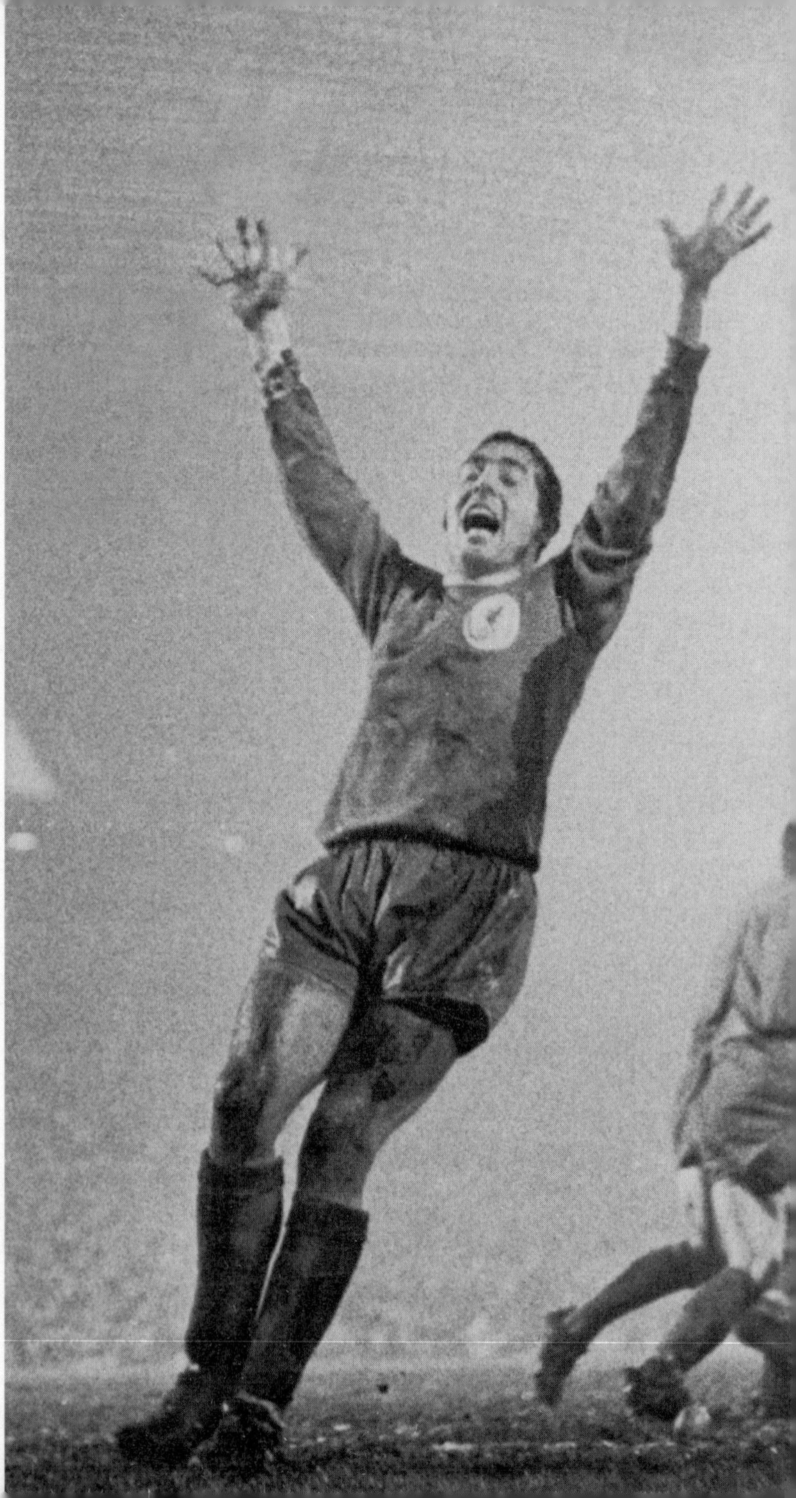

IAN ST JOHN: BORN 7 JUNE 1938, MOTHERWELL; 426 GAMES, 118 GOALS

Ian St John

Liverpool 5 Arsenal 0

League Division One

Saturday 18 April 1964

I ARRIVED AT Liverpool Football Club in the summer of 1961 and I'll be honest; I knew absolutely nothing about them. Not a single thing. I didn't know what they'd achieved, I didn't know who played for them, I didn't even know what league they were in. It seems so strange to think there was a time in my life when Liverpool Football Club didn't matter, but that's how it was. The club was simply sold to me by this amazing man called Bill Shankly. He told me he was in charge of a club that had the best fans and soon would have the best team. In short he told me, no, he convinced me that this club were soon going to be the greatest.

Back then I was mesmerised by him; I didn't know what I know now; that he could sell sand to the Arabs and that I was just another in a long line of players who would fall for his charms. I just sat there that day listening to him selling the club, the place and the fans of this mediocre Second Division club, who had failed to win promotion back to the top flight by finishing either third or fourth in Division Two for the last six seasons. That was a dismal run of failure to win promotion and to break it Shanks had chosen me to spearhead his push for the big time.

I had been doing well in Scotland and was close to signing for Newcastle, who had been a strong First Division team, but they got themselves relegated that season and then along comes Bill Shankly and suddenly I'm moving to Liverpool. No one else could have made me make that move. Shanks was so persuasive, so dynamic.

That vision of a club he wanted to build where the best fans watched and cheered on the best team came to light one spring day at Anfield when we beat Arsenal, no annihilated Arsenal, 5-0 to win the First Division Championship in 1964. That one day epitomised everything that Shanks was trying to achieve at Liverpool. That one match highlighted the buzz in the city, begun by the Beatles and elevated to a new, higher level by us. And, importantly, it showed how a team and its fans could become one. That was exactly what Shanks craved and on that sunny afternoon he got it. It was a carnival day where the supporters cheered us on and we provided them with some sublime football and the trophy they so craved.

That wonderful day was a world away as I drove down from Scotland to Liverpool with Shanks. We talked nothing but football and he outlined his dreams, telling me about every player, how good they all were, and how expert everyone at the club was at their individual jobs. We arrived at Anfield and there was Rueben Bennett, his right-hand man who had been my trainer at Motherwell when I was a kid. I had no idea. Looking back it was all a bit of a *fait accompli*, but at the time it all seemed so right.

I WAS ALREADY a good international. Shanks didn't need to build me up. I had played seven times for Scotland, but instead it was drilled into me just how big Liverpool was going to be. His vision was of a massive club, winning and playing incredible football.

Now it all seems so right. Shanks was spot on. Everything was in place, but at the time only he could conceive of how well we were going to do. The first thing that hit me was just how good the training was. It was amazing. None of us new boys had ever seen anything or done anything like it. At Motherwell we had been used to simple running and it could become boring. We never saw the manager, Bobby Ancell. He was a jacket and tie man, who only turned up on Saturdays, so we took it into our own hands to change what went on in training at Fir Park. There were seven or eight of us young players who had gone full-time at the club having finished school and we took control. Why not? The trainer was treating injuries and the manager was in his office. We had to fend for ourselves - so we did.

We had all seen Real Madrid training prior to their famous European Cup triumph at Hampden in 1960 and just to see those giants of the game was incredible. About half a dozen of us got into their training session and sat and watched and wondered at their skill. They were special. They were doing things with the ball that us young Scottish footballers had never even dreamed of. There we were, wet behind the ears watching in awe. It dawned on us all just how far the game had come from the old emphasis on just running around the bloody track. The skills, the fitness; everything about these guys was unbelievable. Di Stefano, Puskas, Gento, Francisco Kopa; these guys were the best around. They were the guys that set the standards that everybody had to try and compete with. They were so ahead of the world. So when the opportunity came at Motherwell we grabbed the balls, devised our own drills and played small-sided games.

So, when I arrived at Melwood for training it was a wonderful surprise and again, all down to Shanks who had got hold of the place. Outside the new pavilion, Shanks had erected shooting boards of all sizes, we played two-asides on small pitches, it was all work with a ball. Nothing but work with the ball. I loved it. It underlined the neglect in my earlier years at Motherwell. If you asked for a ball back then they frowned at you and said, "If you don't use one today, you'll be hungry for it on Saturday." What nonsense! How can I use the ball when I haven't trained with it? It's like asking a boxer to fight without having sparred.

The playing staff were a good, eager bunch, but Shanks knew he had to make more changes if the club was going to win promotion and start challenging for honours. I arrived, and made my debut in a Liverpool Senior Cup final against Everton at Goodison Park in August 1961. We won and I scored a hat-trick. It was a great start. We then went on tour to Czechoslovakia and when I returned a new but familiar face had arrived; Ron Yeats.

Yeatsie's team in Scotland, Dundee United, had been in the league below Motherwell so we'd never played a league game against each other, but I knew him. We *had* played with each other for the Scotland boys' clubs where he had been captain. We had also played against each other in a game between Scotland's under-23s and the

Army. Ron had done his National Service in the armed forces (I had been in the steelworks to avoid that fate) and we lined up for what turned out to be a right struggle. Literally. We had a little bit of a scrap. He always was bigger than anyone else and really fancied himself. Ron had long fingernails and scratched me down my chest.

I gave as good as I got and Shanks, then manager of Huddersfield Town, was keen on both these feisty Scottish youngsters. Bill later said that if his previous club had given him the money, he would have signed both Ron and myself, but they wouldn't cough up. He wanted Ron at the back and me up front with a young Denis Law. That would have been some team as you have to remember back then, Huddersfield were a far bigger club than Liverpool, and Shanks always used to say that if his board at Leeds Road had been less stingy, Huddersfield would have been the Liverpool of today.

Having said that, he had his work cut out trying to persuade his Liverpool board, who were notoriously tight, to part with the cash. They were by no means the quickest to open the old purse strings, but again, Shanks was able to convince the toughest of businessmen that his policy was the best thing for the club's future. He finally got clearance for what was a lot of money. The most the club had spent prior to me arriving was only £12,000, so the jump up to a whacking £37,500 was immense.

Shanks knew what kind of players he wanted. He knew exactly how to build success and, once the board agreed to play ball as far as money was concerned, he was away. Shanks hated lazy people, he hated those who couldn't be bothered and so he had to have a big clear-out and bring on the young players who were hungry and already at the club.

The likes of Ian Callaghan, Tommy Smith, Chris Lawler, and Gerry Byrne were great. A young Roger Hunt had just come out of the Army and had been sitting in the reserves whilst Tommy Lawrence, the goalkeeper would soon make his way in between the Liverpool sticks. That wasn't a bad bunch to be going on with.

OF COURSE, IT wasn't just the players on the pitch who were vital to the Liverpool set-up. Shanks' backroom staff were imperative to what he hoped to achieve. Shanks had inherited them, but when he arrived he recognised their abilities, did the right thing, kept what was already there and worked with it. That doesn't happen in modern football. Managers today bring in their own "team", their own masseurs, their own tea-lady, but Shanks saw that here was a group of men who were very good at their jobs.

Shanks had no preconceived ideas and simply said "let's work together and see how we all get on". Well, he found out that he couldn't get any better than the likes of Rueben, Bob and Joe and that was it. He had known Bob from their playing days, he'd been keen to sign Joe whilst manager at Huddersfield and Reuben had worked long and hard with Shanks' brother Bob in Scotland. Everybody got on with it. Shanks came in and got that unity from the start.

He used to say that if someone came to him telling stories about someone else, he would frown upon, not the man being spoken about, but the man telling the story. His staff shared that loyalty and they realised that here was a man, a phenomenal football man, who was going to bring success and so they, of course, wanted to be a part of it.

We played some good stuff and that persuaded crowds to return to Anfield and enjoy what they saw. There were always decent crowds at Liverpool. They were getting about 25,000 in the Second Division, but soon the fans, like us players, took to Shanks' ideas about the club and where it was headed.

He got them excited. They felt part of it. He would talk to them even during games. He would say which players he felt were doing well, who was improving and just what was happening. So the crowd soon responded and started to build up to 30,000, 35,000, 40,000 and by the time we won the division, which we did at a canter, the crowd had really begun to swell.

With Shanks at the helm and the players beginning to gel, we won back the thousands of fans who had become disillusioned after eight years in the lower leagues. Those fans truly believed that the club weren't interested in getting back in the big-time and that, quite rightly, upset them. Whether they were accurate accusations I don't know, but now under Shanks they could sense a change and were swept along by his optimism. You couldn't fail to be.

The day we clinched promotion was an ecstatic one. Fans poured on to the pitch, singing and demanding, once we had won the game, that we come out and see them. It showed us all just how much our success meant to them and we knew from that point that we *had* to bring them more and more. Anyway, Shanks demanded it. We all got a cigarette box from the directors that Shanks scoffed at. He said the presents would be bigger and better once we brought the big one - the First Division title - to Anfield.

The crowd really got going and soon you couldn't get in unless you were there hours before a match and the atmosphere at Anfield became electric. We had to get to grips with the new level of football we were playing at, but it seemed fairly natural to us all. Maybe it was because Shanks had kept telling us that we were made for success that we found the step up an easy one. We still had a bit to learn, but it wasn't the struggle that, for lesser teams it can be. Nine wins on the spin from November showed that we had what it took to compete with the best.

We weren't yet ready to be champions though. At Easter, we slumped to one win in nine games to the end of the season after we got beat 7-2 by Spurs, who had a great side of course. They had won the double two years previously and now had my old mate Jimmy Greaves scoring a hatful of goals for them. He bagged four that day. We had beaten them 5-2 at Anfield three days earlier though. And I scored one of those. We'd been two down at half time, but came back to hit five in the second half. That was a great comeback.

Spurs got their revenge with relish, but the story behind that defeat was that the referee couldn't perform on the day and so they got a substitute in who was a local guy and clearly an avid Spurs fan. Dave Mackay handled on the line and he waved play on and then Gordon Milne chests it down in our box and he's pointing to the spot. Shanks was furious. "You'll never ref again in your life!" he shouted and I don't think he did. They may have won anyway, who knows, but it would have been far closer. Years later I reminded Jimmy Greaves about it, but he would never have any of it.

DESPITE OUR POOR finish to the season, our performances against Spurs, who were just about the best on offer in the division, showed that we were ready to compete for the big prizes and we were happy to finish a fairly healthy eighth. The nucleus of the team was in place, but Shanks got on with adding one or two pieces to the proverbial jigsaw. One of those, and I believe possibly one of Shanks' most important signings, was Peter Thompson.

Thompson had turned many heads with his robust displays for Preston. Everton were keen, Wolves were keen, even Juventus had shown an interest, but it was Shanks who got his man, paying another club record fee of £40,000. He was direct, he was fast and he was skilful. Thommo was the entertainer, he was everything. He alone was worth the entrance money. The crowd loved him. He had so many tricks. He would stop, he would start, he would weave.

He complemented our team so much. And now we had a great mix. We weren't just a machine; we had individuals such as Peter who could do the unexpected. He was like the foreign winger, or a throwback to the great wingers of old like Matthews and Finney. It was a travesty that he didn't play more times for England, but he was never going to get a look in, not when Alf Ramsey decided to do away with wingers.

Whilst Thompson was a crowd-pleaser, he also knew how important the team ethic was. Anyone who played under Shanks had that drummed into them. We had great individuals, but we didn't rely on them. What we were trying to achieve, we were trying to achieve together. We would not have stood for a Rodney Marsh type of player.

I'm not knocking Rodney, he was blessed with fabulous talent, but at Liverpool the team came before the individual. At Anfield you couldn't stop everything so you could show off your talents. We were selfless and we helped each other. If you were having a bad game then fine, keep working and others will try and bail you out. We were an honest team and you just didn't get the selfish headline grabbing, glory-hunter that abounds today because Shankly simply wouldn't have allowed it.

Instead what we had was a simple work ethic and plan. Simplicity was Shanks' byword. He always used it. People complicate things. They over elaborate. If you keep it simple then you get results. Give it to a red jersey; you can't get simpler than that. Share the ball. If there are three of you together and one guy out on his own, you don't give it to the guy who's all alone, you share it amongst the group.

Arsenal do that today, they knock it between themselves. It works. Pass and move, that was our style. We trained like that and we played like that. If it breaks down, you cover for someone else. It was all so unselfish. Rodney Marsh would have stood and posed whilst someone worked to get back. Don't get me wrong, I love to watch these type of guys; I just don't want them in *my* team.

I WAS LOVING playing for Liverpool. Not only was the team set up well, the fans great and the staff wonderful, I also had the perfect striking partner in Roger (or Sir Roger as he was later known on the Kop) Hunt. Roger's style suited me and my style suited him. It was as simple as that. He was great.

He was two-footed, hard-running, direct, honest, willing. You would pick it up, he would make the run, you would play it through to him and "bang", it's in the net. He had a tremendous record. In fact he's still Liverpool's record goalscorer with 285 goals in a decade at the club. He would graft as well though. I liked to come deep and pick the ball up and have a look and he was making a great run and he made my life easy.

Shanks had seen just how well we could complement each other and took us both aside to work on making us as effective as he could. He had us training together and so we were always working with one another on different drills and practising different moves we could use. It was a great combination of two talents and two styles complementing each other and I loved being involved in it.

Later in our partnership I dropped deeper and deeper which suited me and I thrived on seeing centre-halves wondering what to do as I hung back. Shanks loved it too. "Take them for a walk, son", he'd say. I would and, of course, Roger would fill that gap and so often be in to score a goal. The great Tom Finney had finished his career in a similar role and Shanks, always Finney's biggest fan, liked the way in which such a role opened up defences.

Having said that, we weren't the only ones scoring goals. A player who didn't receive enough plaudits and who was so unlucky with injury was Alf Arrowsmith. When I was driving down to Liverpool with Shanks after our first meeting he went on and on about this kid. "This boy can score goals," he drooled. It turned out to be Alfie and, of course, Shanks was right. Alfie's goal per game record was marvellous. He played in 20 matches that season and scored a remarkable 15 goals. That was how prolific he was. He was a Manc, mind, but the Scousers loved him all the same. He couldn't always play because of Roger and I, but Shanks occasionally played all three of us and that was hard for defenders. It was a shame as he got injured in the following summer's Charity Shield against West Ham and was never the same player.

WHEN I LOOK back on that great day when we clinched the 1963/64 League Championship against Arsenal and all the great things that went along with that match, it is easy to forget about just how bad our start was to the season. We lost our first three home games that season, the last being against West Ham, who had a fine team, but we always used to beat West Ham! We did win three of our first four away games, but things weren't good and it seemed everyone was doubting us; except of course Shanks.

The board weren't exactly happy. They had invested quite a bit of cash in Shanks' dream, but here we were losing every game in front of our own, hungry fans. They called Shanks in so he could explain what was going on, but he was having none of it and wasn't going to be drawn into a panic. "I can assure you gentlemen," he explained straight faced. "We will win a home game this season." The following week we murdered Wolves 6-0 at Anfield.

With that, the stuttering start was finished. At the end of September we went on a run that saw us win nine out of ten games, which included a win at Manchester United (big Yeatsie got a rare winner that day) and a victory over Everton, who were champions. We really had our tails up and slaughtered Stoke at home and then Sheffield United, both by 6-1. We loved pummelling teams. We would never stop. If we got a big lead we would keep going; that was how it was. Everyone wanted the ball; everyone wanted to score a goal. I got three against the Blades and I still craved more.

Our form continued after Christmas. We had bad days, but we would draw rather than lose and when we reached Easter, a vital point in the season, we went up another gear and that really was that. In three days we won 3-1 at Tottenham, 2-0 the following day at Leicester, a very strong side, and two days later won the reverse fixture against Spurs, also by 3-1. Then the following Saturday we hammered Manchester United 3-0 at Anfield. Alf Arrowsmith was on fire in front of goal, bagging seven goals in six games. Another 3-0 win, this time over Burnley a week later, meant that if we could overcome Arsenal at Anfield, despite having three games left away from home, we would be champions for the first time in 17 years.

It was such a great time to be in the city. What a buzz. You had the docks, the music, the comedy, the nightlife and of course the football, the place was jumping. The fans at Liverpool would pick up on the Beatles songs, sing and sway and put their own words to them. It was brilliant. The day of the Arsenal game, the BBC's *Panorama* came to Anfield to look at this new trend on the Kop, which was viewed as a new social phenomenon. I think it was Richard Dimbleby who quoted the Duke of Wellington, who said of his troops before the Battle of Waterloo, "I don't know what they do to the enemy, but by god, they frighten me."

The crowd could be so funny. I remember that season we lost to Second Division Swansea in the FA Cup quarter-final at Anfield. It was an awful result. We battered them, but their keeper had one of those inspired days. He played like Banks. We just couldn't find a way past him. We got a late pen at 2-1 and Ronnie Moran stepped up. He was usually so reliable, but instead he decapitated a couple of guys in the Kop. If he'd scored we would have gone to Swansea and won, but it wasn't to be. For years fans who were there that day, when they saw Moran, an amazing servant of the club as a player and a coach, would shout, "What about Swansea, Ronnie lad!"

WHILST THE TV cameras were outside studying the crowd queuing up to get in to see us take on the Arsenal, we got on with preparing for the match. Shanks had his own ideas on how we should prepare for a game of football. He was a huge boxing fan; he loved fights. Only a couple of months before, Cassius Clay had won the heavyweight Championship and he loved how brash and how confident this young fighter was. Shanks' favourite though was Joe Louis, and he had heard that the ex-heavyweight champion of the world used to train on steaks. That was it. "If it's good enough for Joe Louis, it's good enough for you lot." We had steaks on the Friday night before games in the hotel, the morning of the game and after the match.

People go on about pasta diets and the right things to eat today, but for us it was steak for lunch, a steak after the match, nothing but steaks. Maybe if we had eaten pasta we would have won the league by more! It's nonsense. It gets people jobs doesn't it? Dieticians, nutritionists, they all get work, but for us and for Shanks it was steaks. If you could pass the ball, eating pasta wasn't going to change that, and if you couldn't pass the ball then eating tons of the stuff wasn't going to improve it.

Shanks, as well as loving boxing and all the old fighters, loved gangster films. He adored James Cagney and stories about Eliot Ness. I think he wanted us to be *The Untouchables*. We would often go to the cinema on a Friday night and Shanks would check if there was a good old gangster movie on. He took us to the USA one summer and we went to play in Chicago. Shanks wanted to see where the Valentine's Day Massacre had taken place and asked a rather embarrassed guide who, of course, had to show him.

Gangsters, boxing, these interests were all there and you could see them in the way Shanks used hype to get us and the fans going. The press loved him for it as he always had a line for them. He was the master of hype and that just made days like this one so memorable and charged the atmosphere even more.

It was electric at Anfield. The sun shone down and the crowd were well up for it. They had to be there by one o'clock otherwise they weren't getting in. Simple as that. Roger (Hunt) had come in early for a fitness test and he couldn't believe how crowded it was outside the ground hours before kick-off. Once you got out on to the pitch, the crowd had worked themselves into a frenzy and the atmosphere was insane.

I guess the fans knew like ourselves that we were on the verge of something special. All the preparation; getting out of the Second Division, feeling our way in the First Division and now we were just one win away from being crowned champions. With Everton having won it the year before, taking it from them was going to make this extra special.

Once we were in our dressing room, you couldn't hear the noise outside. We were quite sealed off, but the away team could definitely hear the racket as they had a window. If you opened it for some air then all that noise and fervour would pour in. I don't think it was a ploy, but, as Dimbleby had said, it must have frightened a few visiting players over the years.

There was no warm up back then, you just got out there. And leaving the tunnel, with that sign above the exit that Shanks had so cleverly put there saying "This is Anfield", that's when the noise hit us for the first time. There was something special in the air that day and as we took to the field it gave us an incredible lift. You would come on and the roar that greeted you as you crossed the halfway line was awesome. Whoosh. It never stopped lifting you, however long you had been at the club. The Kop used to sing my name; *de de de-de-de de de de de St John*! They used the same chant years later for Kenny Dalglish, so they must have reserved that one for the special players! They also sang When the Saint goes Marching In. I loved it. It used to puff my chest right out and my confidence would go sky high.

We lost the toss and attacked the Kop end in the first half. All the photographers were behind the goal we were attacking. I remember there was one lonely looking guy sitting behind Tommy Lawrence in our goal. God knows who he worked for.

Arsenal started the game well though. Ronnie Moran knocked a weak backpass after about 30 seconds and Tommy had to be quick off his line to smother the ball. Arsenal weren't the team they had been decades before, or the one that would win the double in a matter of seasons, but they were a useful side and like most Arsenal sides, very hard to break down. They finished eighth that season and had some decent players such as the Scot Ian Ure, George Armstrong, who was always very lively, and George Eastham. I knew George quite well; after finishing his career a Stoke he went on to coach in South Africa. After I finished in England, I went to play for his club in Cape Town and we won the league down there.

Then; my magic moment. Roger and Alfie did all the hard work and I got on the end of it to slide it into the net and send the Kop crazy. It was a bit of a scrambled effort. It was not one of my best that's for sure. But who cares? It set us on our way. The Kop began to up the volume, but we were almost caught out immediately and Gerry Byrne had to clear the ball off the line within seconds.

We continued to attack the Arsenal defence and both Cally and Alfie tested Jim Furnell in the Arsenal goal. Jim had been at Liverpool in the early 1960s. He was a solid keeper and the save he made from Alfie Arrowsmith was especially brilliant. We had to be on our guard. Arsenal weren't going to sit and watch our party and on the half hour it looked like we had let them back in it when Yeatsie blatantly handled the ball in the box. It was an obvious penalty and there was no fuss from us, not even from the big man.

That snapper must have got the only photo of a great save though from Tommy who dived to his right to stop Eastham's spot-kick. Can you imagine? The Kop went nuts! It was like we'd scored. They always had a soft spot for Tommy.

Ten minutes later we were two up. Peter Thompson went on one of his runs and weaved through the Gunners' defence before crossing it to the back post where I was on hand to head the ball across the face of goal and Alfie nodded it into an empty net. 2-0. Great!

Being two up, we could relax a wee bit. There had been a lot of expectation that day that had caused a bit of tension, but at half-time we knew we could go out there, enjoy the occasion and play our best stuff. When we were in that situation and that mood we were very hard to play against and that's why we could go on and really murder teams.

We would get our wingers going, who were both, whilst different kinds of players, very effective and gave us great balance.

In the second half Peter Thompson tore at the Arsenal defence with his runs, whilst Cally, always reliable and a brilliant passer of the ball, carved them open. Willie Stevenson in the middle was another wonderful passer and he would send Thommo scampering down the wing, where he'd run full tilt at defenders. You'd want the ball off him and he'd be away to the byline. Or you'd yell at him to get the ball over and he'd beat another man! He thrived on it.

The crowd loved it too, of course, especially on a day like this one where entertainment was the word. I recall one of the biggest cheers actually came for an Arsenal player, Terry Neill. Cally had gone down injured and Terry got hold of the ball and kicked into touch. That wasn't done that much back then and the crowd loved a good sporting gesture.

Furnell continued to play well and stopped an effort of mine in the first few moments of the half. Soon though, the goals came. Thompson scored only his fifth and sixth goals of the season in the space of four minutes. The first was a fierce shot whilst the second saw him dribble his way into the box before a deflected shot made it 4-0.

Hats, scarves, newspapers, they were all flung into the air after each goal and on the hour the rout was complete as Roger made it five. Roger must have been feeling left out and he got in on the act with a low drive that this time gave Furnell no chance. There was still half an hour left and we should have scored more, but I suppose we took our foot off the gas and had a bit of fun. After all, the title was ours. This was our day. Our time. We were enjoying every minute of it.

It was carnival day, it was show time. We had all the back heels going, all the flicks. It was great. It was even better to be doing it against a London team. Shanks loved beating the Cockneys. There was a feeling that the clubs in London had the press behind them and that there was this Southern bias. It made it doubly enjoyable when you beat the Chelseas and the Arsenals or the Tottenhams and the West Hams. It was great to give those guys a drubbing. We all took great delight in that, including the Kop of course. They loved it.

Shanks loved it too when we turned on the style. He would say, "Be arrogant, son." That's why he liked Cassius Clay so much, I suppose. He had that same swagger; a confidence that bordered on arrogance. We were catching the ball on our thighs and playing some head tennis and you could see Shanks on the touchline loving every minute. We were giving the public what they wanted and that's all that Shanks ever asked for.

Rueben Bennett was a little more pragmatic. He would have a go at me for back flicks in a game. "You and your bloody flicks," he'd shout. That day though, he had no need to moan. Everything was coming off and we were well in control. Arsenal, of course, were despondent, but you just have to take it. We were the better team and that's how it was. You go through those days. We would later be on the receiving end. Everton did us 4-0 at Anfield the following September and it was a nasty feeling. You have to get on with it and the following year we beat them by five. I scored the last that day. It took us past their four and the Kop were desperate for it.

WE DID TRY and get more against Arsenal, but maybe after the fifth we were showboating a little too much. The emotion of the occasion began to get to us. We did win a penalty though, and Cally stepped up hoping to complete a set of all our five forwards scoring a goal. Ian missed it though, or Furnell saved it brilliantly, I should say. No matter, it kind of added to the atmosphere and a game that had given the fans some great drama.

The whistle went and we were champions. You couldn't hear the thing though. The referee must have blown it three or four times before we knew we'd done it. It was so special. We had come from the Second Division and had quickly been crowned as the best team in the country. Looking back it was the start of it all, wasn't it? The day, the performance, the crowd, it was all that Shanks had hoped for. And now it was real.

The fans were ecstatic. They had been asked not to come on to the pitch and save for a few young boys, they didn't, but they demanded we go around for a lap of honour. Annoyingly the Football League hadn't provided the trophy on the day - in fact we didn't get the thing until the beginning of the following season.

Maybe they didn't think we'd beat Arsenal. So, big Yeatsie has got a papier-mâché trophy off a kid and we're lifting it up to the crowd. That always makes me laugh when I look at the photos now. I wonder if the kid ever got it back. Big Ron was loving it. He kept getting kisses off some of the female fans and was strutting about like Sean Connery for the day.

We made our way to the directors' box and took the loud and long applause off the ecstatic fans. It wasn't the hugely orchestrated occasion that it is today, I mean we didn't even have the real trophy did we, but it was special. A few of us went to the local pub and had a few beers as there was no players' lounge in the old Anfield main stand. Our wives used to sit in the car waiting for us after a game, but Shanks soon got them in his office with a cup of tea. It's all changed now. In the new stand they've got a crèche for the kids and all the babies are there. But back then it was straight home. No big deal.

Strangely we didn't win another of our three remaining games, but that happens. It's psychological. You've done the hard work and you take your foot off the pedal. I was very pleased that Chelsea had clinched the title just days before their Champions League semi-final at Anfield in May 2005. I knew it would affect them as I recalled how we had suddenly relaxed back in 1964 and hoped they would too.

Shanks didn't mind. He knew what we had achieved and he knew that he had got the team where he wanted it. After that season and that afternoon, winning trophies seemed to come easy to our Liverpool team and to the many great sides that have followed us.

IAN CALLAGHAN: BORN 10 APRIL 1942, LIVERPOOL; 856 GAMES, 69 GOALS

Ian Callaghan

Liverpool 2 Leeds United 1
FA Cup Final
Saturday 1 May 1965

YOU WANT ME to choose my most memorable game for the club? Really? I'm going to struggle. I was so lucky to play in so many incredible occasions ranging from our early days in the Second Division to winning championships. Then from those first adventures in Europe there are the wins over Inter Milan and St Etienne and, of course, my last great night in Rome, when we finally became European Champions on an evening that was special for everyone involved with this great club. I was lucky enough to be the only player to span that incredibly successful era of the club, so it's tough for me to pick just one game.

If I have to choose one though, I have to go for our first ever FA Cup victory over Leeds United back in 1965. Success was a novelty back then and to go to Wembley, the famous old ground that we all dreamed of playing at and winning at as kids, was special. The day stands out for me as I sensed we were creating history. The club had never won the FA Cup before and it meant so much to us, to Bill Shankly and of course to the fans. I was a young pro. Aged 23, it was my first time at Wembley and it was a cup we all so desperately wanted to win, so to do it was like no other feeling I experienced in the game.

We had won the league the season before, so we were a confident squad, but with Shanks around and Paisley and Fagan we weren't allowed to become over confident or arrogant about our new success. If anyone was seen to be getting to cocky then they were quickly brought down to earth.

We'd come up from the Second Division having spent what was a lot of money on the likes of Ian St John and Ron Yeats and we had an idea that we could be going places. They were great players and the squad was by now very strong indeed. You knew something was happening. Being part of that squad was special. We all got on so well from the start and that helps. It was as if we all knew something great was happening and that excited us, bonded us together as a unit and created the special togetherness that helped bring the club that initial success.

OUR STRENGTHS AS a team lay in the basics. We had a very decent goalkeeper in Tommy Lawrence, we had big Yeatsie at centre-half, and we had Ian St John at centre-forward. That was our basic spine; those three players and the rest just took shape around that. Our two full-backs complemented each other brilliantly. Gerry Byrne was very hard and almost impossible to get by, whilst Chris Lawler was a wonderful footballer who scored an incredible amount of goals from right-back.

He scored about 70-odd goals in his Liverpool career, which is amazing, especially as he never took penalties or free-kicks. It worked well because, whilst Peter Thompson over on the left wing liked to get going to the byline, I was that bit more of a deep-lying winger. I had no problem sitting back or coming inside and that allowed Chris the opportunities to bomb forward. It was very hard to defend against.

All in all there was a great balance. Other players like Gordon Milne, Willie Stevenson and Geoff Strong were fantastic, so it really was the age-old adage at Anfield, which simply meant getting very good players playing to a very easy system. Shanks had us so well organised and we all knew our jobs. It was all so simple. When we won the league in 1966 we only used 14 players.

Having won the league in 1964, we were on top of the world, but Shanks wasn't going to stop there. He went on to blood some new youngsters, the pick of them being Tommy Smith. What struck you about Tommy was his instant confidence. It is hard to recall Smithy as anything but a man, but he came into the squad as a mere teenager. Mind you, Bill Shankly once said, "Tommy

Smith wasn't born. He was quarried". He was a hard man all right. Tough as granite. And Smithy had all the confidence in the world. You took him for what he was; and he was a fantastic player for the club.

Actually people make too much about how hard he was, and how hard he tackled, but to go on about that is to do a disservice to his ability as a footballer. He was a good player. A very good player. He was and still is a domineering character. He loved to have his say and he loved to boss us around even when he wasn't captain, even when he was young.

We had so many characters in the team, so many leaders, but we all looked up to one man, Bill Shankly. He revolutionised Liverpool Football Club. I still get such a buzz when I go back to Anfield today. It's such an incredible club. The ground is fantastic, the supporters are the very best in the land, the trophy cabinet is bulging with history and silverware and when I walk in through those Shankly gates I always have a smile as I think about the great man. This guy started this all off. He took the bull by the horns and made what was a plodding Second Division side into simply the best.

It was incredible. A lot has been said about the manager and what he did for the club, but it deserves repeating doesn't it? He seemed to know exactly what the place needed and everything he did seemed to work. Even the little things. The details. Having won the league in 1964, during the summer Shanks had a notion to change our kit that was, at the time, the traditional Liverpool red shirts with white shorts and white socks.

There had been talk for a while about a kit change and Admiral had been designing some alternatives, but Shanks said "no" as he felt the new kits simply too upmarket. Instead he just changed the colours from white shorts to an all red. I didn't think about it at the time, but it was a massive change from years of the red and white kit. Shanks got the gigantic Ron Yeats to model them and both of them loved the fact that the all-red kit made Yeatsie look even bigger!

Kitted out in our new colours we went into the 1964/65 season in confident and hungry mood. We were still a young side, so we were still learning, despite being champions. We started playing in

Europe that season. It was so different playing foreign teams and we all thoroughly enjoyed it. We went to Reykjavik and scored ten and that was a huge boost. It was a great and exciting start to the season as champions. Shanks loved everything about Europe.

He would send Reuben Bennett to scout opposition and he enjoyed having to come to terms with new systems and new players. Us players thought the same. It was a break from the normal routine and the same opposition where you knew everybody. There was no squad rotation, no new foreign players. You knew everybody, week in and week out and it did become a little monotonous. So the European games were exciting. We quickly learnt about European football and that began to make us an even better outfit.

MY OWN GAME was coming along. You couldn't help but learn and improve in the winning atmosphere that Shanks had created. He had a wonderful backroom staff and that rubbed off on us all. We had Bob Paisley and Joe Fagan, who was fantastic, and they all complemented each other. Joe was always there for us players. Rueben Bennett was too. If Shanks wasn't speaking to you for one reason or another - usually if you were injured, which he hated - then Rueben would put his arm around you and say "come on lad, don't worry, you'll get over this soon." It was a joy to be there.

I had arrived at Anfield as an old-fashioned wing-half. Shanks took one look at me and because of my height - I was only tiny - realised that I should be wide right. I took to it straight away. I was very quick and I could kick the ball. Joe Fagan told me later that the staff had been amazed by how far I could kick those heavy leathers and that made me an ideal crosser of the ball. For such a little kid that had got me noticed and I had ten great seasons as a winger.

For 73 years the club had strived to win the Cup, and that's what it was back then *the* Cup. Older fans could talk about the loss to Burnley in 1914 and, of course, we had been beaten by Arsenal in 1950, a defeat that had caused so much disappointment, that the Cup had become a bit of a Holy Grail.

Once you got to the final, the build-up was incredible. There was nothing else on anybody's mind. You don't have that anymore. The hype and the interest has waned so much now, which is a real shame.

There was an old wives' tale that stated that if we ever won the FA Cup then the Liver Birds would fly away. We didn't believe that, or the widely held cynical belief that the club was destined never to win the FA Cup. We were too busy to think about all that twaddle. We had to get the players' pool together, give extra interviews and it seemed the fans wanted to chat about nothing else. The final took over really. We had to have our Cup Final suits fitted. None of us bought suits off the peg back then. We would have them tailor-made. Shanks had put us on to a tailor who did suits for Jimmy Tarbuck. For the final though, this local fella, Louis, got the job. He was a real character and came down to Anfield to measure us up. But when the suits arrived some didn't fit, so there we were exchanging jackets. They had the club badge on. They were lovely. I wonder where mine is now? I think we did a song too, but the less said about that, the better. I loved everything about the build-up. There was such a buzz about the city. The expectation was enormous and you realised that you had a chance to make history.

IT HAD BEEN a tricky run to Wembley. We beat West Bromwich Albion. Then we got Stockport, who were bottom of the Fourth Division, but they proved a very hard nut to crack. They pulled off a 1-1 draw at Anfield and Gerry Byrne kicked one off the line, so we were close to going out. We won the replay 2-0 though and then beat Bolton at Burnden Park. I scored a rare headed goal that day. Leapt like a salmon I did!

In the quarter-final we were drawn against Leicester. That was tough. The Foxes were a very good unit, plus they had a certain Gordon Banks in their goal. They had become a bit of a bogey side for us having won at Anfield on their three previous visits and so, despite coming away with a 0-0 draw at Filbert Street, we knew the replay would be tough.

I don't know why we always found it so tough against them. They had some great players like Banks and Mike Stringfellow, but it becomes more than that, it becomes a bit of a mental thing and you grow anxious playing a team that always seem to do well against you. They had beaten us in the FA Cup semi-final two years before, so we were nervous about our chances. That showed in the first game, but we brought them back to Anfield and won by a single Roger Hunt goal. We'd beaten the team with a hex over us, so maybe this was going to be our year.

As I say, we had lost an FA Cup semi-final in 1963 and it was an awful feeling. Not pleasant at all and we weren't keen to go through that again. If you get beat in the final, at least you can say you were there, but to lose in the semi-final is so tough. Now we were up against Chelsea who were a classy, young side run by a young manager, Tommy Docherty. "Docherty's Diamonds", as they were known, were top of the First Division and in Peter Bonetti, Bobby Tambling and Terry Venables they had some of the brightest talent around.

It was going to be tough and was made tougher by the fact that on the Thursday before the semi-final we had to play the German side Cologne in a European Cup quarter-final play-off, as penalty competitions did not exist then. It turned out to be a very strenuous Euro game which we drew 2-2, but won eventually on the toss of a coin. However, rather than being knackered, we were on such a high that we went out in the semi and played terrific.

Willie Stevenson scored a great goal and Peter Thompson slotted a cool penalty and, thanks to the 2-0 win, we were through to Wembley, at last! We loved playing so many games and I think players still do. The more games you play, the less you trained. Not that training is always a good thing!

THE ONLY THING as a pro player that bothers you is injuries and that semi-final almost saw me miss the most important game of my life. I got a knock against the Londoners and was doubtful for the final.

Bob Paisley, our trainer, set to work on me. He had no formal training with injuries, but he had this amazing knack of diagnosing a problem. I was in good hands. We had all the new machines, all the new gadgets, but Bob didn't really know what he was doing. Jimmy Melia was once in the treatment room and they had this new German machine that had you put these little suction pads on and it would bang your muscles around and test their durability. Anyway, they had it on at low level and Jimmy was saying he couldn't feel a thing, so Bob turned it up - but still nothing. Bob nudged it up slowly, but Jimmy couldn't feel anything. Eventually Bob turned it up as high as it could go and still nothing. Then Bob realised it wasn't plugged in; so he shoved the plug in and Jimmy nearly went through the ceiling!

We were going to Wembley where we would play Leeds, who in a way had turned into our rivals. They too were a young team, who had come up from the lower leagues with the help of a fine manager, Don Revie, and were looking to start winning the country's major honours. He and Shanks had the utmost respect for each other. Because of that the hype was massive and the expectation was for a good match.

The staff tried to keep the routine the same as usual, but it was hard amid the blaze of publicity. We were doing interviews and all the talk was of the final, but were aware that you had to keep fit and that you had to keep your form. It was after you played your last league game that you got to focusing on the Cup final as your next game. That's when it got really exciting for the lads.

I was very concerned with that ankle. It was still quite bad and it was only a couple of days before the match that I knew I was going to be OK. It was such a worrying time. I agonised over my fitness, but finally got the all clear and I was overjoyed. It took a lot of treatment though. Mornings, evenings and nights with Bob. Poor Gordon Milne had also been injured and he didn't make it, so Geoff Strong came in. I felt so sorry for Gordon. Even today when I see old footage of the time I still feel for Gordon because he missed out and it reminds me that I was so close to doing the same.

WE CAME DOWN to London on the Thursday by train and Shanks took us to the Palladium that night for a show. That helped relax the lads and take our minds off what we had to do. On Friday it was training and the normal routine. Shanks tried to make it as normal as possible and do things as he would do at Anfield, but it's tricky. You are training in a different place and you know what is around the corner, so you can't help but be aware and feel the nerves.

I roomed with Gerry Byrne in our hotel in Hertfordshire and we both woke up very early on the big day, turned on the television and there was the build-up. That's when my tummy started to go. I tried to have some breakfast, but couldn't stomach much, so we both went for a little walk. You try to do anything to keep yourself calm, but it's bloody hard. We managed some lunch and then the last team meeting.

Shanks never talked much about the opposition and that day he didn't need to. We knew what to expect. It was Leeds and as players we had a lot of respect for them and their strengths. We had played them so much and so we went in knowing what sort of game we were in for. We didn't need Shanks telling us. We had beaten them at Anfield that season and lost at Elland Road, so it was going to be tight.

The boss could go over a few things and just tell us to go out and play our own games. That was vital to our team. We had to go out and play to our system and not worry about them. Of course Shanks had a lot of respect for their players who played the game in the way he liked. Billy Bremner was a favourite of his, Johnny Giles was a wonderful talent and later Peter Lorimer was another Shanks particularly admired.

After lunch we watched some more telly and then we were off on the bus to Wembley. It seems strange now, as we went on to win trophy after trophy, but that day it was all new. Yeah, we'd won the league the previous season, but this was an occasion like no other, this was the FA Cup final and none of us had ever been involved in anything like this. We drew closer to the stadium and the crowds began to swell and then for the first time you see those famous Twin Towers. Oh God, it was magic, it really was. Then the bus goes into the tunnel and the fans are banging on the windows. The Liverpool fans were great and the song that morning was "Ee-ay-adio, We're going to see the Queen!" It was incredible and you knew you were involved in something special.

The first thing we did was check the pitch. The old stadium was massive, the pitch looked enormous and the walk over the dog track to the pitch seems the longest of your life. You take it all in for ten or 15 minutes and then it's off to the dressing rooms to get changed and ready for the match.

Ours was a very relaxed dressing room and Shanks loved that. We had Tarby and Frankie Vaughn come in cracking jokes and making us laugh. It was a gee-up and took our minds off the seriousness of the situation. I think you'll find the Leeds dressing room was a far tenser place that day. They had a young team and maybe we could relax that bit more.

With about ten minutes to go before the game, Shanks told Jimmy and Frankie to leave and it was down to business. Shanks trusted us all to our own routines and that helped. He then got the eleven together and gave us an inspirational speech: "You're going to win because you're the best team," he said, "Leeds are honoured to be on the same field as you. AND you're not going to disappoint the greatest supporters in the world. If necessary - and it won't be - you should be prepared to die for them." We were.

We completed our own pre-match preparations. Everybody has their own little superstitions. Smithy always followed me out the tunnel. Maybe he thought I made him look bigger!

WHEN YOU START to walk out it is like nothing you have experienced before. The buzz, the atmosphere that was the best I have ever heard. The noise, the colour, lining up looking for your relatives. It's special, it really is. We met the Queen, which was a bit of a blur, but I seem to recall she was wearing all red which must have helped. She backed the right horse that day.

The only downer about the whole day was the weather. You usually associate the Cup Final with a bright and sunny May day, but instead it was very grey and would eventually rain heavily. Anyway, you don't think about that too much at the time as the nerves are jangling as you kick off. You just have to get on with it.

It was a tense start, mind, and the trainers were the busiest men at Wembley with many hard challenges in the opening moments. They weren't nasty, but there was always an edge to the games against Revie's Leeds and this Cup Final was going to be no different.

Leeds' midfield hard man Bobby Collins, who'd played for Everton for four years and knew a thing or too about getting his retaliation in early against us, tucked into Gerry Byrne almost as soon as the game kicked off and hurt him. We didn't realise just how bad, but Gerry was obviously struggling. He stayed on as we didn't have subs, though. None of us had an inkling of what was really happening. If you watch it now, Gerry plays the whole game with his arm limp and down. He had broken his collarbone, but he somehow managed to play on. For any athlete to compete with a broken collarbone is a remarkable feat.

Gerry was a fine player. He had been on the transfer list when Shanks arrived. He is now known as a hard man, which he was, but he was also a terrific footballer. People go on about two-footed players or a lack of them, but in Gerry we had a naturally two-footed player. He played right-back and left-back effortlessly. He was just a very good player and a fantastic man to have in your team.

We carried on and tried to get St John and Hunt going. They were always a threat, but Jackie Charlton, who almost came to Liverpool years before, was in imperious form. I myself had an early sniff of goal, but big Jack blocked my goalbound shot.

We were on top in the first half, but the game was far from a spectacle. Both sets of midfield players were very strong and were cancelling each other out. Chances were few and far between, but I felt Leeds were happy to keep the game as tight as possible. It was going to take something special to break them down and Smithy tried his luck from distance whilst the Leeds keeper Gary Sprake saved well from a lively Hunt.

AT HALF TIME Leeds were looking at Gerry Byrne disbelieving that he was still playing. I think they knew how bad he was, but us, his team-mates, just didn't know the full extent of his injury and wouldn't find out the truth until much later.

We could see Gerry was in pain, though, but the management kept it from us. Bob and Bill were like two cunning boxing seconds in as far as they kept him going. They loved their boxing - and its unique approach to psychology. Especially Bill. He used to say to us, "you think you train hard, but boxers, now they train hard. You've got it easy."

Shanks was content with how that first half had gone and told us we were the better team. We were to carry on playing our way and he felt we would eventually break them down. They couldn't defend forever and gaps would soon arrive. The rain really began to fall in the second half, but we remained on top and Hunt again went close with a good header.

I had another shot from close range, but again that Jackie Charlton managed to block it. Leeds were defending deeper and deeper and we had a lot of the ball, but we had to be wary of the likes of Billy Bremner who could turn a game in moments. The Liverpool fans reserved some jeers for Billy, who kicked the ball into the crowd in one moment of frustration.

Gerry Byrne was playing brilliantly. You wouldn't know he had a knock, let alone a broken collarbone. To be fair, our defence wasn't being tested much, but he was everywhere, getting forward whilst blocking and attacking any threat from Leeds. I hit the side netting and it began to look like the game was going to extra time for the first time since 1947.

Big Tommy in our goal was a spectator, but Sprake was in fine form and a late effort by Thompson looked like it might win it, but the keeper was up to it. So, it was an extra 30 minutes. Again, Shanks urged us to keep going. Wembley was a huge pitch and he just kept saying that they would wilt soon. We were always told not to sit down, not to let the opposition see that we're tired, but some couldn't help it I don't think. "Up on your feet", they'd say. I was shattered going into that last half hour.

THREE MINUTES IN and we at last broke the deadlock. It was Gerry, injured arm and all, who got around the back and set up Roger. He nodded in the cross and we were one up. I recall being so elated. A fan came running on to the pitch waving his scarf wildly. He was grabbed by three coppers, but wouldn't stop waving that scarf.

We were thinking "we've done it" and maybe we all took our eye off the ball for a few moments as Billy Bremner soon equalised. I was guilty of standing off Johnny Giles out on the wing. He found Norman Hunter in acres of space inside and his chip was headed down by Peacock for an unmarked Bremner to rocket a half-volley into the far corner. We'd dropped our concentration after we'd scored. Shanks must have been furious with us all. Having said that, it was a terrific goal by Billy. How many times did that happen though? Not many, and we wouldn't make the same mistake twice.

The thing was we were very fit. The equaliser had been a blow, but we were strong both mentally and physically. I think we were the fittest team in the league and, despite the equaliser, we still looked the stronger side. It goes back to how revolutionary Shanks had been when it came to training.

There were only nine minutes left of the match and we really didn't need a replay. We were going well in the European Cup as well, remember, so it was vital we tried to win it there and then. I felt good. I got a second wind. I was up against Willie Bell, the Leeds left-back, and the ball came to me and I was faced with Willie, who was a little isolated. I felt strong and confident enough to knock the ball by him and get after it.

I knew I could beat him for speed, but having played the ball past him, I doubted I could catch it as I had hit it maybe a bit too hard. I hared after it and just managed to get my foot around the ball before it went over the byline and whipped it across. Because of my struggle to reach it I couldn't get much height on the cross, but my only concern was getting it into the box. That was all that was on my mind. The ball was only a few feet of the turf and actually behind Ian St John, but he twisted in mid-air and somehow turned the ball in with a glancing flick. He was a wonderful header of the ball. For his size he was remarkable. He could beat the tallest of defenders who were always shocked by the spring he could muster. On this occasion it was his supple ability to alter his body shape whilst in mid-air that allowed him to score that crucial goal.

Once we went 2-1 up, we simply weren't going to make the same mistake as before. We had to keep switched on. Shanks would never have forgiven us giving up a lead twice in such a big game, but you could see Leeds were spent. Big Yeatsie was Shanks' voice on the pitch and made sure we all knew what we had to do. We had a few vocal players. Ian St John would be doing it from the front. He always had something to say. I doubt he wanted us to blow his big moment. Scoring the winner in an FA Cup final is what we all dream of. Smithy was also giving it to us as well, of course. I was quiet and knackered at the end. In fact the right side of our team was like a monastery. Chris Lawler was the quietest man you've ever met. It was a great combination of different personalities though. That's what made us gel so well. That's what made us tick.

Those last few minutes seemed like ages, but finally it came. The whistle. As it went I just felt such elation. The noise was incredible. I dropped to that famous turf and thought "We've won the FA Cup, and we've done it for the first time". There was so much relief because we'd been hanging on to the lead. It had been such a tough game and we'd come through as winners. It's different from winning the title. That's a great feeling, but the Cup is such a one off. It's a bigger buzz. We made history that day and that can't be eclipsed. We won it again in 1974, which was great, but nothing could better that feeling in '65. Nothing.

IT'S ALL A blur after the game. I have looked back at the footage, but it all seems like a dream. We went up and got the medal. I couldn't say anything to the Queen, I couldn't say much to anyone. I shook hands with the chairman and then it was down the steps and off around the pitch for the lap of honour. We had a few beers and then had a great banquet at the Grosvenor House Hotel. I remember the menu with the Liverpool badge printed on it and going around getting my team-mates to sign it.

Shanks was never one to show his emotion, but, of course, he was elated. He came around to us all individually and you could see what it meant to him. He had brought the title and now the FA Cup to a club he had fallen in love with. He was back to normal soon, though, and went to bed early saying he was off to plan for the next few seasons.

We had to take Gerry to hospital and I helped him on with his jacket. We heard he had broken his collarbone and were just full of admiration. You played for Shanks. He hated injuries anyway. He wouldn't stand for them. If you could play, you would, but what Gerry did was to me the bravest thing I had ever encountered in all my days playing the game.

The train on the Sunday was full of fans. We were in our own compartment and we had to put up a sign saying Gerry was very comfortable, but he won't be playing on Tuesday.

When we returned to Liverpool we went straight to the Town Hall. There were still plenty of Liver Birds in evidence, so we'd scotched that fallacy as well as the thought that Liverpool FC would never win the FA Cup. The number of people there to meet us was amazing. It was a sea of red. We realised that we had brought something to the club and its supporters that they had never before experienced and that was special. The City of Liverpool is football crazy. It's mad and so when you contribute to it in some way it is a marvellous feeling.

In typical style, while we were on the bus after the Lord Mayor's banquet, Shanks let us all know that it was training as usual the following morning as we had a massive European semi-final against Inter Milan on the Tuesday. We stayed together on the Monday night, that was really important. It kept us together in spirit as much as anything and Shanks knew that we had to keep our high going as long as we could. Because of the FA Cup win, the buzz at Anfield for the night of the Milan game was just incredible. The best ever, maybe. That night, St Etienne in 1977 and then the semi-final in 2005 versus Chelsea were the best. It lifts players. When they run out and there is a buzz like that from your supporters, players respond.

Inter Milan were the best team in the world – officially; as they had added the World Club Championship to their European Cup win of the previous season. They boasted wonderful players such as Giacinto Facchetti, Luis Suárez and Sandro Mazzola. To have them at Anfield after we'd won the FA Cup made it very special. When Gerry and Gordon paraded our cup around the pitch, you could feel the ground shake. We were all so up for it. We were terrific. We won 3-1 and it should have been four, Lawler had a perfectly good goal disallowed. The Italians even suspected we were all on drugs!

How could we come off Wembley after extra time and play so well? We were high on life that's how.

Tommy Smith

Liverpool 3 Borussia Mönchengladbach 0
UEFA Cup Final first leg
Thursday 10 May 1973

AT LAST WE'D done it. At last we'd won in Europe and at last Bill Shankly could say he'd been triumphant on the continent. We'd come so close in 1965, when we lost in the European Cup semi-final and then in 1966, when we lost in the final of the Cup Winners' Cup, but now, in 1973, with the second team Shanks had built, we had done it. God, it felt good.

We had been competing in Europe regularly since 1964 and we had been winning Leagues and FA Cups for fun at home, so Europe was the next step and now we'd made it. There was just so much relief on our part, having returned from our European travels with nothing for so long. Shanks was so pleased and I think it started to get him thinking about his own future. There was only the European Cup left, but he said to me he was tired and he missed his family. He had put himself and those around him in the firing line and he had missed out on a lot of their lives. Shanks chose to retire only a year later, content that he'd done all that he could for the club.

I think he felt he could rest in peace once he'd won a European trophy. What a man. There has never been anyone like Shanks and there never will be. He made the club. He took us from a backyard team and made us the best. He used to laugh about how often we were at Wembley. "Bloody hell," he'd say. "Can't we just play these Charity Shields at Anfield and save us a trip."

He was the basis for everything. Shanks had joined the club six months before I made my debut. After getting promotion in 1962, we'd won the league within two years – an unbelievable achievement no one had thought possible. Well, apart from Shanks and us of course. I managed to get my break in the side at the age of eighteen. That was tremendous. To be playing for Liverpool FC for the first time was incredible and actually it is hard to surpass the feeling I got from making my first appearance against Birmingham City.

I was just a kid. Liverpool were my team, they always had been and now I was playing for them. We won 5-1; let me tell you, you can't get much better than that. I was in a right daze that night. My mum and my stepfather went home after the match, but to be honest I just wandered the streets. I walked around in a daze. I lived near the ground, just down the street from the Anfield Road end. No one stopped me mind, they probably didn't recognise me to be honest, but who cared, I was just in my own happy world.

We won having played a lot of kids in the team that day. Birmingham and Manchester United were trying to stay up and, when Shanks revealed his selection, United complained that we were trying to get them relegated, which was a load of shit. We won 5-1 and didn't hear any more from the Mancs on the subject. Having got a taste for it, I just wanted more and more.

MY OWN EUROPEAN career kicked off because in October 1964 England had played Belgium and found it tough, only managing to draw 3-3. The next month we drew Anderlecht in the European Cup. They were a very decent side and boasted numerous Belgian internationals from that side that had given England a run for their money. The management took us away for the night to the Blundellsands Hotel, I was in the squad, but thought I was just making up the numbers. Ronnie Moran said to me, "I think you're playing tomorrow, lad." I just laughed. Before we were due to go to the ground we had a meeting as always and Shanks is naming the team. It came to number 10 and he says "Tommy Smith". I couldn't believe it. "What's going on?" I thought. "It's a massive European game and I'm in at number 10?"

Shanks said we were going to shore up the defence and I would be Ron Yeats' right leg as a second centre-half. Ronnie never could kick with his right. Great player, the big man, but no right foot.

I had played up front and at inside-forward as a kid so could use the ball and I played well that night. As I wore the number 10 on my back, I had their right-half marking me. But I was actually playing at centre-back. "What the fuck are you doing up here?" I asked their number four. I don't think he understood my accent, though! Everyone thought that it was Alf Ramsey in 1966 who started playing with two centre-backs. That's a load of shite, it was Shanks and Liverpool in 1964.

We won 3-0, which was terrific. They had a decent inside-left and in the first few minutes I tackled him hard. I mean I really whacked him, I got stuck in. He came down with a crash and as he got up he said "Loco" putting his finger to his temple as if to say I was mad. I just laughed at him and thought to myself "If I've upset an international player, I've arrived". Me, an 18-year-old; I can handle this I can.

That was me in the team. Shanks must have liked my attitude. We travelled to our next game at Burnley and usually the twelfth man carries some of the kit. We got off the bus and I went to pick up the kit hamper, but Bob Paisley says, "Leave that alone Smithy, you're playing." We won 5-1. It was the perfect kick-start to my career.

IN MY ESTIMATION, that team of the mid-1960s was our best. St John, Hunt, Callaghan, Thompson. They were wonderful players and built the modern Liverpool. By the end of the decade though, that team was getting on and something had to be done.

We had lost some games and we weren't winning cups and things had to change. Big Yeatsie wasn't playing much, so Shankly called me in and said "You're captain, son." That was during the 1969/70 season just before the FA Cup quarter-final defeat to Watford (that I missed through injury by the way), a defeat that really made Shanks' mind up.

Shanks didn't talk openly about it, but you could see he wasn't happy. It was a sad time and no one could really hide how they felt about it. Things weren't right. There were arguments, constructive ones, but arguments all the same. We all wanted success, but realised changes were going to have to be made. In goal, Lawrence went, St

John left, as did Hunt. Legends, all of them, but it was time for new faces. It was time for a new team.

Shanks didn't want to change the system though. He liked to keep it simple. If you were a goalkeeper, he didn't expect you to score goals. Your job was to stop them. Simple. Right-backs, stop the left-winger, centre-backs stop the centre-forward. We'd had Cally, Gerry Byrne and Thompson, who you gave the ball to if you wanted to rest. Willie Stevo, Gordon Milne. They were fantastic. What a great team, but now it had to change and, when it did, those great players were simply and brilliantly replaced by more great players.

Ray Clemence came in and turned out to be one of the best keepers of all time. Byrne was replaced by Alec Lindsay who was a very good full-back. He looked like a midfield player, but he ended up as a great defender and a great crosser of the ball. Just ask John Toshack.

Then you've got the two centre-halves, Larry Lloyd and myself. Larry was solid and, alongside me, helped make our defence the best in the top flight for seven consecutive seasons from 1970. A record I'm dead proud of. Cally was still running his bollocks off on the right wing, whilst Peter Cormack was a class player and could get unfair criticism at times. Emlyn Hughes was at left-half. Crazy Horse would run all day. We didn't get on off the field, but who cares? At outside-left was Stevie Heighway. Stevie was like Thompson, but far more direct. Up front you had Keegan and Toshack; a small forward playing off the bigger target man. It was the same system as the '60s and that's why it worked. There was no complication. Different players, same methods, same success.

Suddenly the team is different, but in so many ways, the same. We lost to Arsenal in the Cup Final in 1971, but gradually the team gelled and won more domestic honours. All Shanks had done was change player for player. He did it over one season really. You didn't even notice it. You were playing with Roger Hunt one minute; the next a young lad called Toshack is playing and scoring. As a player I didn't give a shit as long as I was in the team. There were certain players I preferred to be alongside, of course there were, but ultimately I didn't pick the team and who could doubt a man like Shanks?

No one who had been around him for all those years, that's for sure. Those who hadn't, soon found out the hard way. No-one ever talked back to Shanks, but that changed when a young Steve Heighway gave it a go. I was captain and we would go to meetings and I'd say to the lads, "Whatever the boss says to you, just take it and put up with it." In 1970 Steve arrived and we went down to Crystal Palace and lost 0-1. Palace, I mean we just didn't lose there. Our punishment was to come in for training on the Monday, which we usually had off. We were at Melwood in the dressing room and no one is saying a word, which is the best policy. Steve is young and so, when Shanks walks in calling us a "shower of bastards", he begins to twitch. I'm saying to myself, "Don't Steve, don't you dare". Shanks continued, "You got beat by a crap team, blah blah blah." Then, from nowhere he says, "I'm going to blame Stevie Heighway!' That was it. "Yes, you. Do you realise you lost the ball in their half, and they broke and scored."

"But I'm playing outside-left, how was it my fault?" asked Stevie.

"When you lost the ball you should have turned into a defender."

"I don't think so, that's why we have defenders, to defend."

We're all like, "No, Stevie", with our heads in our hands. Shanks goes right up to him and asks, "If your neighbour's house was on fire, wouldn't you grab a bucket of water and try and help put it out?" Stevie thought about it and said, "When you ask a sensible question, I'll give you a sensible answer."

Oh my God. We couldn't believe it. Shanks blew up. He went mad for ages at us all. I got hold of Steve afterwards and said, "Hey lad, you may have letters after your name, but as far as I'm concerned you are a stupid bastard." To give him credit, he learnt quick. He never said a word again.

WE HAD A system that worked. We were a unit, but that didn't mean we didn't have our fall-outs. You can't get on with everyone. Take Larry Lloyd for example. He was a strong player, a good player, but would accidentally on purpose hit the forward he was marking early on. Nothing wrong with that, but the problem was he did it once in training – against Ray Kennedy, who took offence to his tackle. Larry was a very boisterous guy and Ray couldn't believe it. Larry was sold eventually. He didn't really settle in Liverpool, I don't think he got the team's work ethic. It took Clough to get hold of him and calm him down. Even at Forest he was a bit of a renegade. He won trophies there too, mind.

I remember Keegan once bounced up after a bad tackle and went for him. Kevin was fearless. He came up to Larry's waist, but still had a go. I intervened and Larry started on me. I said, "Please do not get me going, because you will not survive, lad." He walked away. As I say, you can't get on with everybody.

The team ethic was everything and couldn't be upset. I remember people's surprise when it was reported that Frank Worthington was coming to Liverpool. He didn't strike the public as a Liverpool man. A brilliant footballer, but perhaps not right for our team. Us players weren't bothered, "if he comes he comes". He did come to Anfield in the early 1970s for a medical, but failed and was sent away and told to come back another time. Shanks was clearly keen on him, but when he returned a fortnight later, he failed it again. We were confused.

"What's wrong with him?" We didn't know. Anyway, he never signed and months later Shanks was having a laugh with us and one of the lads said, "Hey, boss. What was wrong with that Frank Worthington?" The boss' face screwed up. "Don't talk to me about that Worthington fella," he yelled. "I'll tell you one thing. No one's playing for my Liverpool who's got the fucking pox!" We didn't know then what he meant by it, but, now I've read Frank's autobiography, I've got a fair idea.

Shanks had created his new team, but he continued to make us all feel so important and inspired. I had missed out on two England World Cup squads under Alf Ramsey and only played once for my country, against Wales in 1971. I was disappointed, who wouldn't be? The boss called me into the office. "Tommy, this idiot in charge of England. I can't believe him. You are playing great week in week out and I can't see how you're overlooked. Fuck him!"

That was inspiration. I left that office eight foot tall. I ended up winning titles, FA Cups, European Cups and finished my football a very happy man. Shanks had made winning trophies for Liverpool the priority, and England didn't matter one bit to me.

WE WENT INTO the 1972/73 season really wanting to start winning trophies again. Shanks' new team had found its feet and we could get on with bringing more silverware to Anfield. We won the league again sure, but the memories, that season, lie in Europe. Back then you had the European Cup, the UEFA Cup and the Cup Winners' Cup. Everyone had the UEFA Cup down as the inferior one, believing it the also-rans' cup, but that was wrong. It was the hardest in many ways because it was between the up-and-coming teams; clubs who are about to challenge for the big honours.

It was no coincidence that Liverpool beat Borussia Mönchengladbach in the UEFA Cup in 1973 and then Bruges in 1976, when we won it for a second time, and then went on to meet and beat the same teams in the respective European Cups of 1977 and 1978. That was because the UEFA Cup was about the new teams. You look at the Champions League today, it's not always the Champions that win it, but a team on their way to success.

We got started by beating Eintracht Frankfurt 2-0 on aggregate in the first round. It wasn't spectacular. They simply weren't good enough to beat us. Next it was AEK Athens and again it was very easy. Greek football was poor. We won 3-1 out there and 3-0 at our place and so we were again off to Germany in the third round and we were comfortable 3-1 aggregate winners against Dynamo Berlin.

And yep, it was Germany again in the quarter-final; this time Dresden. What a shit-hole. What I remember about that trip was how worthless the East German money was. Bob Paisley went out for a walk with one of the club's directors and soon this director needs to go to the toilet. He couldn't wait and so they found a loo in this store and Bob is keeping watch so no one goes in. "Bob, could you find some paper?" asked the Director through the door.

"There's no one here," said Bob.

"I need some paper."

Bob went off, but could find nothing, so what he does is slip a few East German marks under the door for the fella to wipe his arse.

In the semi-final we faced Tottenham. It was a big game, but didn't have anything like the hype of the all-British Champions League semi-final in 2005 when Liverpool beat Chelsea. Tottenham were then an ageing team, but had some great players such as Alan Gilzean and they'd knocked us out of that season's League Cup on the way to winning it. We could only manage a 1-0 win at Anfield in the first leg thanks to an Alec Lindsay goal and knew it would be tough in London. That second leg was just was the hardest game and Spurs may have felt aggrieved that that they didn't go through, but we deserved it as we really worked our nuts off. We lost 2-1 down there with Martin Peters getting both for them, but Stevie Heighway managed to grab us that vital away goal and we were in the final.

AND ONCE MORE we were to play a German side, this time Borussia Mönchengladbach coached by Hennes Weisweiler, who had led his team to successive Bundesliga titles in 1970 and 1971. Shanks admired the German way of playing. They played to a system, and they didn't ever stray from that. They stuck to what they did best and he liked that. But we always did very well against the Germans. We always have.

As everyone knows, Germans are tough to beat. They'd had it over England internationally ever since the World Cup Final of 1966, but German players were in awe of how hard it was to play against us at Liverpool. We would keep going and going. They liked playing against the Mediterranean teams, but not us, who just kept coming, whatever the score.

Mönchengladbach were a new force in German football. They housed several internationals, who would a year later be winning the World Cup for their country. Bertie Vogts, Rainer Bonhof, Günter Netzer, Jupp Heynckes. These were fine players and we knew we would have our work cut out.

We were at Anfield for the first leg and, after we'd played for less than half an hour, a rainstorm came down like you couldn't imagine. It banged down like stair rods, but the water wasn't soaking into the ground. You'd kick the ball and it would only go about a foot. We didn't pester the ref to stop it, but there was no football being played, just a lot of splashing around.

After a few more minutes the game was abandoned, but there'd been enough time for Shanks to notice certain things and make some crucial changes. It showed what type of manager we had in Bill Shankly. He saw that the Germans had a defender who wasn't at all keen on heading the bloody thing. Shanks had started with Brian Hall up front, but for the rematch the next night he brought in the giant Welshman, John Toshack.

Brian was understandably devastated, but then so had John been the night before. John went about moaning about the decision without knowing that Shanks was going to change things. That was Shanks' job. He spoke to them both. He never hid. It was nothing to do with me, but I felt for Brain. What I realised from that was Shanks didn't need a full match. He had the Germans sussed from about 25 minutes of sodden football.

Eventually we got started. First of all, it wasn't one of those electric Anfield atmospheres, not right away. There had been a lot of confusion from fans when the first game ended up being abandoned about what they were going to do the next night. Could they come along and get in? They kept their stubs, but some would have just stayed all night and all day, that's Liverpool fans for you. That's how much winning in Europe meant to them. And it meant the same to us players.

I soon realised that what Shanks had noticed was spot on. From the off, the Germans had a problem with Tosh's ability in the air and, with Kevin buzzing around him, we had them on the ropes. After 20 minutes, Lawler sent in a cross, Tosh nodded it down and Kevin flung himself to head the ball in. It was classic Keegan and Toshack.

They had an amazing relationship. That was their forte. Kevin was super fit. He wasn't the most elaborate. I played with Pele in the United States and he could do anything. Kevin didn't have that sort of talent, but he worked so hard and made himself as good as he could humanly be. He had ability, but his fitness kept him going. He was lightning fast, with a great change of direction.

Toshack was wonderful in the air, but also had a great touch and could kill the ball dead. But airborne he was almost unplayable. He was physically strong, like a bull, and he could hold himself in the air. He was brilliant at hanging there and, ask any defender, they hate a forward who can do that.

A few minutes later we won a penalty. We had missed a few that season and Kevin had this one saved too by Kleff. It rattled us a bit and the Germans began to push forward, settling in to the game. They passed the ball about us and then from nowhere Danner smashed the ball against Clem's post.

We had to be wary, but we knew we could still cause them problems, especially as Kevin was in no mood to let his penalty miss ruin his evening. On the half hour, Tosh again got his head to the ball in the penalty box and knocked it down to Kevin, who again was on hand to score. By now the atmosphere had built into the kind of buzz that makes Anfield such an unbelievable place to play football. It inspired me to hear the passion and excitement of our fans; my fans. I loved every minute of it.

We were two up at half-time, but Shanks warned us not to get comfortable. He was proved right early in the second half when Wimmer raced clear, but skied it when he should have scored. We needed another goal and got it through Larry Lloyd, who headed home a Keegan corner. It proved just how much the Germans struggled with our aerial threat.

That could have been that, but Mönchengladbach just didn't stop. They clearly felt that if they could get an away goal then they would be right back in it. With 25 minutes left, Stevie Heighway made a clumsy challenge on their winger, and the referee pointed to the spot. Heynckes, who had been fantastic on the night to be fair, stepped up in front of the Kop and knocked a great penalty into the corner, but there was Clem diving to his right and turning the ball around the post. What a save! The Kop went nuts. That was the loudest cheer of the night.

We were the better team. We felt like we had stuffed the Germans and things were rosy. 3-0 up, sweet. But that can be dangerous. There was always the apprehension that they could get one early on and would be back in it. And ask those Milan defenders from

Istanbul, who wants to be in the team that lets a three-goal lead slip? Shanks was aware of it too. His basic chat after the game was, don't lose your concentration. "This was the first half; there is still a lot to do." Typical manager-speak really.

WE WENT OUT to Germany with the usual trepidation about travelling abroad that we'd had since 1965 when we lost the second leg of the European Cup semi-final in Milan under, let's say, suspicious circumstances. Shankly, when it came to European opposition, wasn't likely to trust anyone, and I for one didn't blame him.

These teams started on you as soon as the plane touched down. In 1965 we arrived in Milan, having won 3-1 in the first leg, and there were people at the airport screaming at us. Then when we get to the supposed sanctity of our hotel we're right next to a flaming church. A church! Shanks went to the priest and said, "Can you please turn that bell off?"

"No," said the priest. "It's been here for over 150 years."

"Well, can't you put it a rag around it?"

We got to the San Siro, there were fireworks, the lot and then the ref's been got at and he's giving them everything and they beat us 3-0. We were heartbroken. The whole thing was an outrage, but there was nothing we could do about it.

From then on Shanks didn't trust anyone. So, as soon as we arrived in Germany he was on his guard. Our wives came for that trip and had a bit of trouble from the locals, which put us on edge, but Shanks was always wary. "They can't play as badly as they did in the first game," he said. "I know we were in command and we took the game to them, but it is now their turn to do the same to us." And how right he would be.

As captain it wasn't hard to get people geed up. If you weren't up for a game, you didn't play for Liverpool. Simple as. The management wanted to see effort. Your ability is there otherwise you wouldn't be at the club, so it was endeavour the backroom looked for.

It was clear from the off that the Germans were ready to have a go at us. Günter Netzer was on fine form, as was the winger, Rupp. I remember he went over the top and did my shin. "Little bastard", I growled and I knew it was going to be a tough night. I didn't wear shin pads and that bloody hurt, that one, I don't mind admitting.

Their crowd was incredibly noisy. The Germans made some good chances early on, but squandered them. Then, on the half hour, Cally underhit a pass which Rupp was on to, he darted to the byline and pulled it back for Heynckes to score. The volume again went up to a mad roar. The ground was very much like an English stadium with the fans very close to the pitch and that made it quite an intimidating place to be. The German players were rising to their fans and with five minutes left of the half, Heynckes scored another goal. This time curling the ball into the top corner. Clem had no chance.

In that situation you think your world is about to cave in, but you have to focus. I pulled a few of the lads together and got us defending much higher up the pitch. They had pinned us back and we had to change that. Shanks was going barmy, getting us organised, wanting us to defend over ten yards rather than forty.

WE WENT IN at half-time and Shanks by now was very calm. He wasn't ranting, that would have been wrong. "Look, boys. Calm down, take control", he said. "This lot have put in a lot of energy and they can't possibly keep that level of workrate up. It's going to be a different second half."

Joe Fagan put his arm around me and said "Smithy, take control, sort it out, get them organised." As captain it was down to me to sort things out on the pitch. He pulled me to one side and said "Smithy, somebody needs marking. Delegate." That was a vital half-time break. We were happy to get in, reorganise and have a think about how we could stop them playing.

As ever Shanks was right. They were spent and we knew early on that they didn't have much more to offer. As the half wore on the Germans didn't have much of the ball and they couldn't attack. The crowd were silenced. Every game away from home in Europe we were told to shut the crowd up. Once that happened you knew you were on top. The first half had been a mad noise, but the second was quiet only for the odd boo and they were directed at their own.

Their players began to give the ball away very easily and we began to make chances. We really should have scored a couple. Phil Boersma came on and missed one or two good chances. We could have drawn the match, to be honest.

I knew with ten minutes to go we'd done it. Those closing stages should have been hair-raising, but they weren't. We were in control. Netzer had been so good in the first half, but he'd disappeared out of the game. He'd put too much in. We made sure we had someone on him so as much as he wanted the ball he couldn't get it and as that went on the energy drained from him. They had to go sideways rather than forward. Even Cally was marking their outside-left, Rupp, who had made the first goal and caused us loads of bother. We'd all put in the effort.

When the whistle went, the first thing I saw was Shanks jumping for joy! You didn't see him do that much, but it showed just how much he wanted to be victorious in Europe.

We'd won the UEFA Cup - I think we were the sixth consecutive British club to win it - but there was no big ceremony. They pulled the smallest little rickety table out to put the trophy on. Talk about basic! Today there's fireworks and confetti, but back then there was nothing. What I remember most is how fucking heavy the trophy was. It has a stone base that one, and when I got hold of it I could hardly lift the thing.

After a while our supporters got on to the pitch. There I was with this massive, heavy trophy and this big fat fan grabs me around the neck to celebrate. There I am with the two heaviest things in the stadium and I'm struggling, I really am. I remember I said to this lad, "if you don't let go of me I'm going to break your fucking neck." Those were the first words out of my mouth after I lifted Liverpool's first-ever European trophy.

ABOUT FOUR OR five years ago I was in my local supermarket. This woman came up to me and said, "Are you Tommy Smith?"

"Yes."

"Do you remember playing a game in Germany, the second leg of the UEFA Cup?"

"Of course I do."

"Well, do you remember a big lad grabbing you by the neck trying to hug and kiss you?"

"Yeah, of course I do."

"Well, he's over there," she said.

He was too scared to come over so he had sent his missus. I looked over and laughed. "Did he tell you what I said to him?" I asked.

"Tell me? He's never got over it!"

I took the cup off the pitch. In fact I always seemed to have it because no one else wanted the thing, they couldn't lift it! I got into the corridor outside the dressing room and I'm sat on the flight of stairs and Shanks says "Come in, Tommy. Join the party." But I couldn't get this thing any further, I was too knackered.

What was great and what stands out for me was Joe Fagan coming over to me. Joe was such a lovely man. He was almost my mentor at the club. He had looked out for me when I was a kid. He could be bloody strict though. I would do all the jobs; the boots, the ground work, painting seats. Anything that needed doing us kids had to do it. I was about 17 and the day I signed my pro forms, the other boys were all sitting around together. I was playing the big man. "After I've signed this form" I said, "I won't be doing any of that crap again. Stuff the kits, stuff the dressing room, they can clean themselves." I went in and signed my forms. Having done it I've gone into the dressing room and I have my back to the door. The other boys asked me what I was going to do now. "Nothing", I said, "I told you". "Brush the table, lad", I said to one of the apprentices. "Hold on, you've missed a bit." I was really rubbing it in. What I didn't know is that Joe's standing behind me and I wondered why the lads are giggling. I thought they were laughing *with* me. I've sensed someone behind me and there's Joe. He had a face on him! My God, he had a face on him. He never said a word. He just looked at me; he just gave me one of his stern looks. Well, without hesitating I picked up a brush and got sweeping!

So, coming off the pitch in Germany, Joe's come up to me and said, "Tommy, that was the best game you've played for us lad. You were magnificent. I know we got beat, but you were spot on tonight. When we went two down you were our voice out there. Brilliant, lad." Joe wasn't one to give plaudits, so when he said that I thought, "Christ, I must have done well."

I was so proud. To be captain, to be a Liverpool winner and to be a European winner was everything. I was in the first Liverpool team to win the FA Cup in 1965, the first to win in Europe in 1973 and the first to win the European Cup in 1977. Not bad that. I fucking loved it.

We may have got beat, but looking back I am proud of the way I marshalled the team that night. It was a verbal display in many ways, but that pleases me. At the time all I was doing was my job. I was captain and I had to demand stuff off of the lads. I went a bit far sometimes, threatening people - ours as well as theirs - but to me I had to be cruel to get the message across. Sometimes you'd get the odd response like, "Let's see after the match, Smithy", but nothing ever happened. We were mates and we all knew the score. We all just wanted to win at any cost.

We could have become shell-shocked at 2-0 - like Milan did in Istanbul. We realised that if we didn't start playing like a team instead of individuals were we going to get beat. They had taken advantage, but once we started to perform like a unit then we were so very hard to play against. That's how Rafa Benitez' Liverpool enjoy success in Europe and that's what we did in the second half that night against Mönchengladbach.

There was no mad party. Just a few beers, but we all had a good warm feeling. We hadn't been shown much respect out there before the game and really we just wanted to go home. There was such a big sigh of relief that we were too tired to go mad. It was tame. We had lost the game, remember.

Shanks made us love winning and it became a wonderful habit. What incredible days. Winning became a wonderful habit. We travelled the world and were loved pretty much everywhere we went. My father died when I was 14 and I was a fan because he was. Now I was skipper of a team winning all over Europe. I wouldn't change my time there for anything. I would love to be playing today and be earning the big money and anyone who says differently is a liar, but the time, the fans, the music, the players and Shanks. You can't get better than that.

Lives must be so empty to those who dislike football because the game introduces you to so many strange people and takes you down so many weird roads. It's wonderful. Take our fans. I used to meet some right characters. One day I was having a cup of coffee before a European trip and this fella comes over and sits next to me at the airport. "Alright, Tommy," he says.

"Alright, lad."

"You're my favourite player," he says. We got a bit of banter going and then he says, with a deadly serious face. "Me and the wife have had a conversation, and you are our favourite player. I've come here to the airport especially to ask you a huge favour. Could you sire my next baby?"

"What do you mean?"

"You know. You and my missus."

"You must be joking."

"No, no, Tommy, it's alright. We've had a conversation and she is OK with you siring our next baby."

"I think we'd better leave this pal. I'll sign anything you want but sire your kid? You must be joking."

PHIL NEAL: BORN 29 FEBRUARY 1951, IRCHESTER; 648 GAMES, 60 GOALS

Phil Neal

Liverpool 3 Borussia Mönchengladbach 1
European Cup Final
Wednesday 25 May 1977

THERE WE ALL are, sitting at breakfast, none of us having had any sleep. It's the morning after the night before and us players are on top of the world, well Europe, but you know what I mean. The jokes and the singing haven't stopped and then there's Bob, making his way into the dining room. He looked like he always looked. He had on his old cardigan, full of holes, his old slippers are on his feet and his tabloid newspaper's rolled up in his back pocket. This morning though, there was something different. Something extra. In his arms was the European Cup and he wasn't going to let it go. I'll never forget that sight. We all just looked and marvelled at the man who had made us European champions; we just stood and let out a huge cheer.

It was, to coin a phrase, the best of times. To go out to a city like Rome and to win the European Cup for the first time in the manner that we did was magical. The team, the fans, the match, everything was perfect and it's a night that everyone involved will always cherish. I know I will. We'd had an amazing season and hoped to win all three trophies still up for grabs at the end of it. That wasn't to be as we lost the FA Cup Final after winning the League, but with Bob Paisley at the helm, we knew that it was about time we made this famous club the Kings of Europe.

It had been a tough start though, for both us players and for Bob himself, who had struggled to live up to the legend that was Bill Shankly. I joined just a few months into Bob's first season. I watched the lads get knocked out of the Cup Winners' Cup by the

Hungarian side Ferencvaros and things were clearly a struggle. Bob admitted to the lads in that Durham accent of his that he "didn't want the bloody job anyway."

Things weren't running smoothly. Bob was finding his feet and, of course, what didn't help was that Shanks would be turning up at Melwood, making his presence felt and in a way confusing all those players who had played under him. To them he was "The Boss", but to Bob, Joe and Ronnie it was like having Bill on the bench with them and something had to be done. He had to be shunned by some of the men who had worked with him so closely for so many years. Those same men now had to get on with building for more success, constructing Bob's team.

THAT'S WHERE I came in. I was Bob's first signing in the October of 1974. I was 23-years-old, but had been playing for Northampton since the age of 16. I had over 230 games under my belt and had caught the eye with plenty of goals from midfield where I played at the time. Part of me felt that my time had passed and at 23 maybe I wasn't going to get a move to a big club; I was wrong.

Newspapers used to rant on about this goalscoring midfield player from Northampton, but I wasn't sure if any of the big clubs were paying much attention. Bob Paisley was. He sent Geoff Twentyman, his chief scout, down to the Cobblers. Geoff had an incredible record when it came to spotting talent and was responsible for a conveyor belt of brilliant players making their way to Anfield. Kevin Keegan, Ray Clemence, myself, and later there was Ian Rush. He was great at that and he came along to see me, but I ended up playing two-thirds of the match in goal. Liverpool were planning to spend £60,000 on me and there I am standing in between the sticks. We won the game, mind, and I kept a clean sheet, so perhaps that proved my versatility. Anyway, Geoff must have liked what he saw.

At the press conference to announce my signing, Bob said that he hadn't seen me play, but he knew I could play in every position across the back four and was naturally two-footed. That would do him and that gave me great heart. I realised that ability might just win me my chance.

That opportunity came along quicker than I imagined. I had only played four reserve games when I got my first break and what a game to start with. It was a Saturday morning and I was all prepared to play for the reserves, whilst the first team had a derby match at Goodison. Tom Saunders, Bob's advisor, came round to my digs that morning and said there was a problem with one of the full-backs so Bob wanted me to join the first team squad.

I was a little nervous, but I thought, "Part of the squad, OK, that's fine". We went to Anfield to pick up my boots and I asked if we would be taking the car and Tom is like, "No, that won't be necessary. We'll walk across the park." So there I am walking to Goodison with my boots in a brown paper bag amid thousands of Scousers all asking me for tickets. This is my first experience of the Merseyside derby, remember, and I couldn't believe how electric the atmosphere was.

I was just enjoying taking in the whole day, enjoying the occasion, but then I walk into the dressing-room. "Get ready, son," says Bob. "You're playing." "Bloody hell". I never had a chance to phone my Mum or anything. I went out in front of the crowd and I thought, "If I can cope with this then I can cope with anything that life throws at me", and I did. That day was my base.

We drew 0-0 and I jumped for joy, cuddling Emlyn Hughes like we'd won the league. There's 56,000 fans thinking "Who the heck is this fella?"! It was a great start for me and was an early hint at the genius of Bob Paisley. Bob hadn't allowed me to dwell on the fact that I would be playing in a Merseyside derby and so told me at the last minute. He was so clever was Bob. He was always thinking ahead.

I appreciated that I was around some great players and I had to learn to have confidence, not arrogance. I played at left-back as I had for the first 18 months of my career and got on with it. That derby game gave me a bucketful of confidence and, although I went back into the reserves for a couple of matches, I managed to break back into the first team and then didn't miss a league match for nine years or so. Life didn't get much better than playing for Liverpool Football Club. Ray Kennedy was coming through, Terry McDermott was fighting for a place, soon local boys Jimmy Case and David Fairclough would arrive and Bob's team started to take shape.

THAT FIRST SEASON of Bob being in charge finished without any silverware. We ended up as runners-up to Derby in the league, but I was soon taught that that isn't good enough for Liverpool. I was quite excited by being a runner-up in the English First Division and looked forward to picking up some sort of medal. "Oh no, you don't get them, son." Don't be ridiculous. Liverpool did not celebrate finishing second. You don't get congratulated for falling below the highest standard. What you do get is inspired to win it the following year.

I was learning so much. I trained hard and kept my head down. I was lucky to be next to Cally in the dressing room, who was a brilliant example. Get in early, cup of tea, don't be rushed, train well and play well. I learnt all that from Cally, which was great, but generally I kept myself to myself, to start with that is.

The following season, 1975/76, was vital but is mostly forgotten because of what subsequent teams went on to achieve. We won both the league title and the UEFA Cup with a side that had quickly gelled and become very hard to beat. We had to win our last game at Wolves and were struggling at 0-1 down, but managed three goals in the last 15 minutes and the fans went ballistic. I think that night in the Midlands was the start, that was the moment the fans knew, the players knew and Bob knew that things were back in place. Bob began to act like *the* manager. Bill's ghost had been laid to rest.

That meant we were in the European Cup for 1976/77 and we were desperate to go one better and win the biggest prize of all. We were a confident bunch, but had to endure a strange pre-season with all the talk about whether Kevin Keegan would be staying or going. That continued on for the entire campaign with what felt like daily paper-talk about Kevin's destination abroad. We knew he was off, but the whole thing could be a little distracting. Kevin became the butt of a few jokes and Smithy wouldn't let up, calling him "Concessions Keegan."

We'd all arrive at Melwood on a Monday morning, but no Kevin. "What supermarket is he opening this morning, Bob?" Smithy would ask. "What formation next week, Bob, 4-4-1?" Tommy was senior enough to get away with that. He was a man of the city and it upset him that sometimes Kevin was out busy doing other things.

I admire Liverpudlians for that. They are bold enough to say it how it is and that's what Tommy did.

We were told that Kevin wanted new challenges in Europe, but we all knew that deep down he wanted to double his wages. No one minded that, but I would have liked if he had just come out and said it. When Souness left in 1984 he just met us all and said, "Lads, I am going for the money. See you later."

It was light-hearted with Kevin though and the team got on with playing well and winning honours. By Christmas, when we knew that Keegan was definitely off, we were challenging for everything and actually wanted to give him a good send off. The European Cup was well under way and we were looking good.

We had started out playing Crusaders, the champions of Northern Ireland. We beat them 2-0 at Anfield and they were ecstatic at that result. It seemed the whole of Northern Ireland came out to see us in the second leg and thousands were scaling lamp-posts, drain pipes and trees to try and get a glimpse of us. We were in the dressing room and there were loads of people trying to get in and have us sign autographs. This is before the game, remember, and Bob's face was a picture.

"Get them bloody out of here, Joe! Fucking get them out." He was worried that this game wasn't finished yet and didn't want us feeling as if we were playing a friendly. As it was, we went out there focused and won the game 5-0. Next was Trabzonspor in Turkey. I missed the first leg through an injury. Bob Latchford had given me a dead leg in the derby game the week before and it sounded like the big man did me a huge favour. Thanks Bob.

Tom Saunders had come back from his scouting mission saying it was bit dodgy out there, but the lads returned, having lost 1-0, effing and blinding about what a terrible place it was. The worst they'd ever seen. They were well pleased with having only lost by the one goal, that's how bad the trip had been. I played in the second leg and we won 3-0.

SO, WE WENT into 1977 looking forward to a quarter-final against St Etienne. They were a class outfit, they really were. The tie has gone down in Liverpool folklore. We lost out there 1-0, but the night at Anfield will never be forgotten. The intensity of that night has only been matched by the recent game against Chelsea, both were so similar and both were testimony to what football means to Liverpool's supporters. We scored early through Kevin, but Bathenay got a vital away goal for the Frenchmen before half-time. Ray Kennedy then put us ahead on the night, but we still needed to score again to go through.

The game is rightly remembered for David Fairclough's goal. What a player David was. People have gone on about Solskjaer, but Fairclough was the original "Supersub". I played 450-odd consecutive league games and I don't think David got 450 minutes, yet he'll always be remembered because of that night.

St Etienne had some great players such as Dominique Rocheteau and what has been forgotten about that night is that we still had about eight minutes to play once David had scored his fantastic strike to make it 3-2 on aggregate. For those eight minutes, the French battered us. They really came at us and we were hanging on. Fingernail stuff. We were kicking them off the line, there were critical tackles, Clem last-ditch saves, the lot. It was incredible. That was the only game that my concentration went from the field of play to the stands. The noise, the movement; people didn't want to sit down and were twitching about they were so nervous. If we had not won that night we might never have seen the great river of success that followed.

The semi-final was a bit of an anti-climax, but we had to be wary because the Swiss team FC Zurich weren't bad. We noticed that they, like German teams, could be pulled about at free-kicks, so we worked hard on that in training. They were so rigid in their marking that you could be clever and that's what we were. Jimmy Case and I worked on a free-kick and it came off out there early on and I got in to score. We won 3-1 in the first leg with me getting a second thanks to a penalty and you could tell that the boys on the journey home were desperate to start planning for the European Cup Final.

That, though, wasn't allowed. We had to bite our tongues, as the management weren't ever going to allow any complacency. We kept our heads and won comfortably 3-0; 6-1 on aggregate. And that was that; we were off to Rome. It was a mad few weeks. We won the championship again, we got to the FA Cup final and we were planning for the biggest game of our lives. There were a lot of meetings. Suits had to be fitted, tickets allocated and songs recorded.

IT WAS DOWN to Wembley first for the FA Cup Final in which we got beat. It was strange. Not a lot went wrong that day apart from the fact that we lost 2-1. Tommy Docherty actually said his Manchester United side had played shit and won that game. We may have won it if Bob had picked the eleven that would play in and win the European Cup, but we had so much belief in ourselves and such a great team spirit that we just had to get on with things.

Bob built his team around people who could captain the club: Clem, Smithy, Thompson, Kevin, myself, Emlyn, later Souey, Kenny, Ray Kennedy. That was Bob's idea, he knew that the more players who were mentally strong and who were natural leaders the better for the team, and that night, after losing the FA Cup, we all had to be strong.

So there we were at Harrow station, a group of players who had just been beaten by their arch rivals at Wembley in a showpiece final. We should be gutted but it was Clem - who had been so disappointed by the result and his own display - who suddenly went "Fuck it, let's get pissed," and starts dancing there and then on the platform. That was that. The journey home turned into a party with the wives and us players enjoying a drink and a giggle. We had Jimmy Tarbuck on board, who set the tone and, after some drinks, some laughs and some bonding, the United slip-up was out of our minds. We had the European Cup Final against Borussia Mönchengladbach of Germany to think about in a matter of days. Onwards and upwards.

Having slept it off on the Sunday we trained hard on the Monday at Melwood before boarding our Aer Lingus flight to Rome on the Tuesday, all decked out in our dapper new suits and ready to go to work. The wives and girlfriends flew out separately and enjoyed a day and a night out in Rome whilst we went to our hotel, had a light training season and got our heads down for a good night's sleep.

The morning of the match is when the nerves start and the build-up begins. I roomed with Clem and I woke him for breakfast at 9am. I was always waiting on Clem. I used to tell him he could play until he was 40. He never had to move on the pitch and I was doing everything for him off of it. I waited on him and got him his papers and toast.

We had a light stretch and then returned to the hotel for lunch and a final meeting. The lunch was the usual fare. Fish, chicken or steak and some beans. What there always was, was plenty of toast. No bread, no rolls allowed, just stacks of toast. You could have 300,000 pieces of toast, but no bread. I never did work that out.

It was 1pm and time for the team meeting. If the lunch had been our usual menu, Bob's meeting certainly wasn't. Bob never did go on too much about the opposition, but that afternoon he didn't mention them at all. He sat us down and started going on about the war. "The last time I was in Rome, I was in a tank liberating the place," he said. "I took on the Germans back then and you'll do it tonight." We were in hysterics laughing, but a part of me wanted to know about the winger I would be marking. The Dane, Allan Simonsen was European Player of the Year that season and a dangerous player. How should I play him? Who knows. Instead Bob was telling us how hard he had worked in the war to give us youngsters a better world and now was the time to repay him.

Bob knew what he was doing, though. Right at the end he went on to tell us how we would be playing and it would transpire that Bob's tactics were spot on. Mönchengladbach had been destroyed in the UEFA Cup final of 1973 by John Toshack and feared his ability in the air. Bob knew Tosh would miss the game through injury, but kept him in the squad just to keep them on their toes. Kevin would be on his own up front, pulling the defenders all over the place, whilst Stevie Heighway would work off of him. Terry Mac was to interchange with Stevie Heighway, whilst Cally would hold the centre of the midfield.

As for telling us about the opposition's strengths and weaknesses, Bob wasn't one to dwell, and anyway he could never remember people's names. He would use the word, "Do-ins" when he couldn't recall individuals. We never knew why he used that word, he just did. It was "Watch do-ins out on the left, he's tricky," or "Get at Do-ins at right-back, he's had a knee injury." He had so many quirks, Bob. He once said to me, "Phil, watch the winger, he's not quick, but he's nippy." He'd say this team tend to "Ponk" it. "What's Ponk?" Smithy would ask! He never did get a straight answer. That was Bob. Somehow he got his point across.

Having had our "chat" we went to our rooms for an afternoon nap. I loved those and had no problem, however big the game, dropping off. Clem and I slept and then it was downstairs for some tea and of course some more toast, and then it was on to the bus and off to the famous Olympic stadium for the final of the European Cup.

WE ARRIVED AT the beautiful stadium and went out to check the pitch. It was then that it hit us just how many fans had made the trip. We knew they had spent money on the journey to Wembley and had heard that they had sold fridges and cars, or anything to raise the money to make it out to Rome. It hit us when we walked out and saw that incredible sea of red and white and more flags than I've ever seen. Stevie Heighway came over to me. "Phil," he said. "Look at that, mate. We have to win for them. We have to win tonight for all those people out there."

I remember the pitch was very hard, but luckily the studs I had worn all season were quite worn and perfect for the surface. Soon though, you're in the dressing room and nothing else matters. It's time to get out there and make history. We walked out (it's a bloody long walk at Rome's Olympic Stadium) alongside the Germans and all I kept thinking was how tall their keeper, Wolfgang Kneib was. Look at the size of him! He was about three inches bigger than Clem, who wasn't small. He's towering over us all and I remember thinking then "If I get a penalty, I'll have to keep it low".

We prepared to kick-off. We stood there waiting for the whistle and you could tell that all that disappointment from the weekend, all that depression was gone and, amidst that sea of red and white, we were ready.

Early on everyone was getting good confidence-building touches and it became clear that Kevin was going to give the great Bertie

Vogts a torrid night. He pulled him all over the place and Vogts began to get annoyed, tripping Kevin up left, right and centre. I myself was keen to get going and felt good early on after I managed an important block from a Heynckes shot. From then on I was always wanting the ball. Whenever Clem had it he always looked to bowl it out to me.

That was an unsaid thing. Clem picks up the ball, I peel to the touchline to receive it and start something off. That night I would have Cally always showing inside saying, "If I'm tightly marked, don't worry. Give it to me and I'll give it back. Let's move them about a bit." It was a European style of football. We could dictate the pace of a game and that's exactly what we started to do.

I was enjoying it. "Come on, Jimmy," I said to Case, who was ahead of me on the right flank. "You and me, let's make this Simonsen worry about us." We had a lot of the ball and I was enjoying getting forward. It was great having Jimmy there. He didn't mind doing all the kicking and grafting in front of me and that would leave a lot of room for me to bypass him and get into the opposition's half.

We had to be careful, though. Just after the half hour, Rainer Bonhof, a great player, strode into our half and unleashed a shot, that to be fair, beat Clem. But it struck the upright. It was the only sniff the Germans had in that first period, whilst we were looking dangerous each time we got near their penalty box.

Ray Kennedy brought a good save from Kneib, whilst Case had a shot cleared. We were happy with how it was going, but, just before half-time, it was about to get better. It was a tactical night. It was in many ways Bob's win and the goal that put us ahead was perfect in its execution as it was exactly how Bob had hoped that we would open them up.

Kevin had been told to be "The Lone Star" up front, taking Vogts away from the central area and out on to the flanks and his decoy run was ideal. Stevie Heighway drifted in with the ball, saw Terry Mac's run from deep and slipped it through, Terry received the pass and bang, goal. It was absolutely perfect and showed what a master tactician Bob was.

We were on top, but during the break we were told to be wary. "Hang on", the management said. "They're going to have a go at us and we have to be on our guard." Unfortunately, it wasn't long before we were forced to listen as it took Mönchengladbach only minutes of the second half to draw level.

It was a mix-up between Jimmy and myself. He thought I was further back than I was. I'd started to go on ahead of him and Jimmy passed it straight to Simonsen, who battered the ball into the top corner. I was right behind it and I knew it was in straight away. It was a huge blow, but I had to get on with things and make sure Jimmy's head didn't drop. He needed cajoling as he was down about the goal. He was very quiet and had gone within himself. They were mounting attacks down our side and so I'm saying, "Come on Jimmy, it's gone. Let's get back on this."

From then they really put us under pressure. Clem made some fine saves, one brilliant block from Stielike and I recall thinking, "Bloody hell, I'm glad he's here tonight." People forget we were under the cosh for a good while and Clem saved us twice with world-class goalkeeping.

We were working hard, but Kevin and Stevie weren't getting many openings. They ran tirelessly, but could they still hurt the Germans, whose real Achilles heel was in the air? Some would have been forgiven for thinking the answer to that was "No". It was going to be up to one of us to exploit the space they were trying so hard to create; but who? We'd all been pegged back as the Germans pushed forward

HAVING SOAKED UP a lot of pressure, we won a corner. I was just glad of the rest when Smithy, who never went up for corners, said, "Cover me, Phil, I fancy this."

"Alright, Smithy, no problem. Up you go."

Bob always afforded us that freedom. There were no rigid rules about who went where at set-pieces and if you fancied it, then up you went. So off went Smithy.

Who would have thought it? In what was supposed to be his last game (he eventually went on for another season at Anfield), Smithy connected with as good a header as you'll ever see and we're 2-1 up. Brilliant! It was his testimonial on the following Friday, so he obviously felt if he scored the winning goal he might get a few more fans in and line his pockets a bit. Typical Smithy!

We might have been leading again, but the Germans weren't going to stop getting at us and they soon had us under the cosh. To help, Kevin dropped back into our half and he picked up the ball deep and he went on this diagonal run at Bertie Vogts. It took the ball and the pressure as far down the field as possible and was just what we needed. What a clever run, Kevin. He just went and went and went, with Vogts nipping way at his heels. Eventually Vogts was forced to make a challenge that the ref saw as a foul. Penalty!

Fantastic! You'd have thought so wouldn't you? The ref points to the spot and my first reaction is "Oh Christ, it's all on me now!" I'm 50 yards away and I have to make what felt like a hell of a long walk to the penalty box. There's eight minutes left and if I score, it's all over. If I miss…

Emlyn looks at me with desperation in his eyes, Smithy looks at me with one of those, "Score this or I'm breaking your fucking back" stares and Cally, who had never been booked and is so quiet and polite, shouts, "Hey, Nealy, stick this in will ya.'

I was very confident when it came to penalties. I had done a book with Clem on the art of taking and saving penalties so I ought to have known about scoring them. One of the rules was vital - don't change your mind. I look at the keeper, pick the ball up and I'm thinking "Come on, this is my turn. Keeper's left, keeper's left," I'm telling myself as I put the ball down. As I turn and run up I've changed my mind. Blind panic. I did the same in the FA Cup against Brighton in 1983 and missed, but this time God is on my side. The keeper goes the other way and the ball's in the net.

It wasn't until I got home and saw the photos that I noticed as I was running up to take it Cally, who had played 800 odd games, is praying; literally standing on the edge of the area praying for me to score. Bloody hell, there was a lot on my shoulders. That goal meant a lot. If I had thought about the numbers of people that wanted me to score that penalty, the number of fans whose lives almost depend on your success, I probably would have missed.

The bench were going crazy. Fairclough, Tommo, Tosh, Alan Waddle. They were all so happy with my penalty. I was so elated and so relieved. Wolfgang Kneib, I will always remember his name, his height and his eyes as I went on that run-up.

After that the legs felt good. We were all full of running. Terry Mac, especially, was covering acres. He could go all day, even after ten pints of lager. He was a great athlete. Tommy Smith was coming to an end and his will to win urged us on. Cally had been there since the start and his quiet but professional attitude was so vital to all of us. Whilst Kevin was off to Hamburg and we wanted to give him something to say "Bye". Joey Jones was so passionate, so hyper and such a lift in the dressing room. He had been a fan and it showed.

We all wanted it so much. We had proven our worth. Mentally we had been so strong. We were so gutted to lose that FA Cup, but now we had won the biggest prize of all. The whistle blew and it was just sheer joy. I went straight to Clem and hugged him. 'What a year, mate.'

SO, IT WAS time to celebrate. We had put so much in both physically and mentally that season and now was the time to let our perms down and party. The press were there, the fans got into the Holiday Inn and it was mayhem to be fair. The food went like locusts had got to it, but it didn't matter. You never fancy any food after a match anyway. We didn't mind, we wanted to share it with whoever. A load of Scousers at a free party. You can imagine, can't you? The food went, the ale went, it was magic. At about two o'clock we all went to Stevie Heighway's room and carried on there.

By morning we were all around the pool and, footballers being footballers, people were soon being thrown in. I had bought some new shoes from Russell and Bromley for about £80, which was quite a few quid back in 1977, and Kevin is trying to get me in. "I've got a shitty watch on that I don't care about that, but let me get my Russell and Bromleys off," I cried. Kevin was having none of it and in the struggle I caught him under the eye with my thumb. Kevin came home with a real shiner and the press were adamant that Smithy had hit him, but it wasn't that at all, it was me trying to protect my new shoes.

It's really when you return that you realise how many people you've touched. Millions of fans are there to say "Thank you" and that is special. We want to say "Thanks" to them because their role in our success was vital. Ask today's players, they'll tell you. Liverpool got through tough games against the likes of Juventus and Chelsea to win the 2005 Champions League because of the fans and the desire they transmit from the stands down on to the pitch. The footballers today know and so did we.

It was a wonderful summer. One I'll never forget. It was the Queen's Jubilee year, Virginia Wade won Wimbledon and then there was Bob. A simple man, but a brilliant one. I can't believe he didn't get a knighthood that summer. It was such a privilege to be around him. I never missed a day's training because I loved it so much. Heavy cold? I'm in. Slight knock? I'm in. I didn't want to give them an excuse to rest me and I didn't want to miss a day with the players and the staff.

It was such a fun place to be. There was so much laughter, so much joking about but, my God, once we crossed that line, there was nothing but a dogged determination to win. Wherever we went, be it Poland or the Nou Camp there was always a belief and a drive to be the best. It was like Bob had built a Roman army and sent us out to conquer Europe.

ALAN KENNEDY: BORN 31 AUGUST 1954, SUNDERLAND; 356 GAMES, 21 GOALS

Alan Kennedy

Liverpool 3 Tottenham Hotspur 1
League Cup Final
Saturday 13 March 1982

PULLING ON THAT famous red shirt and going out play in front of those fans was the greatest thing a footballer could do. I had so many wonderful memories, so many incredible nights and so many glorious victories that it is hard to choose one. I guess most people would automatically presume that I would choose the night I scored in Paris to win the European Cup or that evening in Rome when my penalty won that same famous trophy. They were great occasions and I'll always cherish my contribution to each and every one, but if I had to pick a game that always stands out for me personally, it would be the 1982 League Cup Final when we beat Tottenham Hotspur to win the Milk Cup. That was the game that made me believe that I was, at last a treasured part of Liverpool's starting XI. That meant so much to me.

That will surprise a lot of people. In the spring of 1981 I burst through the Real Madrid defence and scored a goal that made Liverpool European champions for the third time. I was, of course, on cloud nine, who wouldn't be, but soon, and this was typical of Bob Paisley and the club, I found myself struggling to get into the team. One minute you were a match-winning hero, the next you were warming the bench.

As I tried to fight to get back into Bob's plans, I picked up a niggling hamstring injury and getting back into contention took a lot of hard work. Slowly but surely I did it though, and in March 1982 at Wembley against a quality Spurs team, I had one of my best games for the club. And we brought more silverware back to

Anfield. The League, or Milk Cup as it was known then due to its sponsorship by the Milk Marketing Board, may have always been a second-class citizen in terms of the honours available in the game, but that particular year, it became a sought-after honour for us. Very important as it proved to be a victory that confirmed that not only did I have a good future in the game, but so did Liverpool, Bob Paisley's new Liverpool.

Again, that may sound odd. How could people have doubted the team's place in the game? We were Champions of Europe after all and boasted players such as Kenny Dalglish, Alan Hansen and Graeme Souness. That wasn't enough for some of the pundits though. We had finished fourth in the First Division in 1981 and had started the next campaign erratically to say the least.

WE OPENED THE season with a 1-0 defeat at Wolves and we also lost at Ipswich. Manchester United and Southampton beat us at Anfield and things were looking, let's say, disjointed. On Boxing Day 1981 we got beat at home by Manchester City and I was on the bench. That was a serious low point. Not only did we get beat, we got done 3-1. We were awful and, despite Bob building a new young side, the vultures were out declaring the end of the era. The dynasty was supposedly over.

Bob had invested money in certain new players. One was Mark Lawrenson; others were Craig Johnston, Ian Rush, Steve Nicol, and Bruce Grobbelaar. Great players eventually, but they were settling in. Bob had taken apart his old team and we waved goodbye to Jimmy Case and Ray Clemence, whilst my old drinking partner Terry McDermott would soon be on his way. Liverpool always brought one or maybe two in, but that year Bob brought in four or five new players and they were all learning together at once.

It was always going to be difficult, but none of us expected to look at the league table at Christmas and see us sitting at 14th. That was embarrassing and Bob, along with his staff had to take action. We would always have team meetings and Bob called one on a Friday morning to discuss things. He wasn't pressing the panic button, that wasn't his style. He had too much confidence in his ability to spot a good player to worry too much about our poor form, but he felt it was time to iron out why we were losing so many games and letting in so many soft goals.

Everyone had their say, but it was clear that these youngsters were trying too hard to impress and finding it hard to get to grips with the Liverpool way. Rushie hadn't shown any of the form that would make him a legend at the club in years to come and Brucie in goal, well Brucie was all over the place to be fair. We'd got knocked out of the European Cup in Bulgaria and he'd let in a soft goal. I can see him now, coming out to claim a ball he had no right to and it's sailed over his head and the outside-right has an open goal. That was a blow.

Bruce, though, worked hard at his game. He was a great trainer, he was very athletic, very fit, but he was prone to these messy errors. Joe Fagan said to us defenders, "When he comes, all of you get on the line. Expect him to come for everything." They knew, though, that they had a gem of a keeper and he proved it and won more championships than any other goalkeeper. A bad player doesn't do that. Back then though, he had to learn the basics. Ray Clemence had gone to Spurs and now Bruce didn't have an experienced man there to learn from and so he had to teach himself and that was going to take time. The thing was, he was a natural.

THE TEAM HAD a lot to contend with up to Christmas and so did I. In 1981, as well as that goal in Paris I had scored in the League Cup final against West Ham. I had been paraded around as this god. Bob, Ronnie and Joe saw this and decided that they would have to be careful so as to make sure that all the publicity and adulation I was getting wouldn't go to my head.

Maybe it had a little, I don't know, but they thought it would take four or five months to bring me back to earth. Bob decided to leave me out of the team, he bought Lawro late that summer and he could slot in at left-back which meant Phil (Thompson), Alan (Hansen), and Phil Neal could remain across the back four. The thing was that meant I wasn't getting in. I played here and there, but mostly I was on the bench and when you play for Liverpool, the bench isn't a nice place to be.

I was really annoyed with the way Bob and the staff were handling it. I was getting quite irate about the situation and I called a meeting with the manager to have it out. I made my way to this meeting determined to put my point across and let them know how angry I was. There I was standing outside the office, waiting to go in and give the manager a piece of my mind. "I need to be playing, Boss, I need to start games and I need to start games now!" It was all set up in my mind.

He kept me waiting and stewing for ages. Then I walked into the office and my bottle went. I froze. Rather than being all forceful and commanding like I had planned, I humbly asked if there was any chance of getting back into the team, anytime soon. Please!

Bob was quiet, but he had a way about him and he could be intimidating if he wanted to be. He just said that I needed to keep working and eventually I'd be back in the set-up. Paisley was a genius. I was outside his office wanting to be angry, but I ended up apologising for not be up to his standards. He knew that the team was a little unbalanced, but I think he was making sure I knew my place in the squad. Brilliant. I worked hard and I listened. Having scored the goal in Paris, I thought that would be enough, but it showed that at Liverpool no one was assured of a place.

I, though, was settling down. I had a girlfriend, who has now become my wife, and at 28 was reaching my prime. From then on I was going to listen to Ronnie Moran and do what he told me, give my best in training and concentrate on the football.

AFTER THE CITY defeat we went to Swansea in the FA Cup and I was handed my chance. Bob brought me in at left-back and we played well, we won and I thought to myself, "I am never going to be dropped from this team again". I had to get used to new players, though. For so long I had played behind the classy Ray Kennedy, but he had now gone. Ronnie Whelan had come in and was a different kind of player.

Kennedy knew exactly how Liverpool played and was always so simple and tidy. Ronnie arrived as a young man and was very flamboyant, very confident. He would try anything, flicks, deft touches, the lot. If it didn't come off, then so be it. That was novel to me and not quite the Liverpool way of doing things.

What *was* the Liverpool way was the ability to resist sentiment. At the beginning of the season Graeme Souness had replaced Phil Thompson as the team captain. Tommo was devastated, he loved the club and had just lifted the European Cup, but the team had started badly and changes were made, it was as simple as that.

Thompson, like so many ageing great players and servants, knew he was on borrowed time. Just prior to Christmas we had played in Japan in the World Club Championship against Flamengo of Brazil. I travelled all the way out there, but was left out. Bob played Mark at left-back instead. We went 3-0 down at half-time and I'll admit that I was laughing to myself thinking, "that's what you get for leaving me out". Looking back I may not have made a difference, Zico was absolutely brilliant.

Bob might have realised that day that maybe now was the time to change the centre-backs. Phil might have begun to look a bit slow or whatever. It was a combination of things and the City defeat seemed to be the last straw. There was a new back four in Bob's mind and it seemed like the right time to start blooding it. That was myself at left-back, Mark and Alan in the middle and Phil Neal on the right.

Tommo still had a role to play for a while yet, but Bob was starting to fashion his options into the unit he hoped it would become. The rest was history. Manchester City went top of the league on Boxing Day and we were 14th. By the end of the season, we'd won the Championship and City slumped to finish tenth.

We went on this incredible run of wins to take the title. It was great to be involved. I remember the games and the way we played. I was loving it because I had set myself a challenge to get back into the team and cement my place and I was living up to it. Things were good again.

We went unbeaten for our last 16 games, winning 13 of them. It was awesome. That poor start had been banished and slowly we started eating into the lead set by the season's frontrunners. Other teams knew that we would come strong in the second half of the season. That frightened them. Ipswich had a great side but they could see us getting this head of steam up and they began to lose games. It affected them. Aston Villa won the European Cup that year and Ipswich were UEFA Cup winners, but no matter. Once they saw us playing so well they began to fret and we took the title. They were great opponents though. You'd think bigger clubs like Manchester United and Arsenal would be challenging us, but they were no more than great pretenders back then.

BOB'S YOUNGSTERS WERE starting to shine. Rushie wasn't at his best yet, Whelan and Johnston were learning, but slowly their talents began to blossom. Who could doubt Bob Paisley's judgement? Plus there was so much experience, Kenny, Souey, Hansen, Neal, myself, it was a good mix.

These guys had to learn the Liverpool way. Give the ball to a red shirt, move into an open space, expect the ball back and that was it really. Those teaching you knew know more than you and you had to listen and learn. Rush started to score, Johnston's energy and eye for goal was winning games and Ronnie Whelan was becoming the player who would be Mr Consistent for Liverpool for the next ten years. As for Brucie, those forays, whilst never completely vanishing from his game, were kept to a minimum and he became far more dependable.

As for me, I was now injury-free. I had been plagued by that hamstring problem for about 18 months, but it had now gone and I was desperate to cement my place in the team. I became so consistent and I went on to play a total of 140 consecutive league games. It was massive crossroads in my career and one I will always look back on with fond memories.

Our fans thrive on similar memories and more often than not they revolve around trips to Wembley and winning cups. As I say, back then the League Cup was a big deal for Bob Paisley's Liverpool. It was silverware after all and now Bob took it seriously, which hadn't been the case previously, and the club would go on and win it for four years on the spin. That's a record which I don't believe will ever be broken.

We'd put together a good run in that year's competition, beating Arsenal early on and then Ipswich in the semi-final 4-2 on aggregate. Bobby Robson's Ipswich boasted the likes of Terry Butcher, John Wark, Arnold Muhren and Paul Mariner. They were our main rivals for the league, so that was a big win.

We were off to Wembley again. One of my first games for the club was in 1979 at the old place against Arsenal in the Charity Shield. We beat them 3-1 with Kenny dummying David O'Leary and lofting the ball over Pat Jennings. "This'll do me," I thought. We were brilliant.

We were always there though, weren't we? We'd laugh about it. "Oh, we're going back to Wembley," we'd mock. "We have to go down there again, do we?" But for me it never lost its buzz despite it being our second home. We wouldn't be blasé mind; we were just taking the mickey.

We recorded our usual crap record. Typically we got bladdered with drink and sang this song about how we drank milk. Nonsense, but great fun. Those were fun times. As we were doing better on the pitch, things were getting easier off of it. Rushie had come in and, whilst he was painfully shy at first, he was now more comfortable amongst us all. Ronnie was always confident and great to be around, whilst Brucie was just his mad self. There were a lot of jokers. When Bob spoke we all listened intently like, but we knew how to have fun.

We'd have to get serious though, because Spurs were a good team. Any team that wins successive FA Cups has to be a tough side to face. They had so much flair and you always had to be on your guard against them. Glenn Hoddle would be relishing the big, open pitch, whilst Ossie Ardiles, Steve Archibald and Garth Crooks were among the finest players in the country. We had shown earlier in the season that we were fallible and I'm sure the Londoners went into that game confident of another trophy.

But for us that League Cup final had a lot riding on it. There was a big onus for the club on winning it because it could give the young players a taste of success and prove that this new team might just become as successful as the previous ones. It was a significant year for everyone.

It was vital we win. Bob wouldn't have put any extra stress on us, he never did that, but within the squad there was a real feeling that if we could win then we could kick on and continue to be successful. We were at the beginning of that run that would clinch us the title and, looking back, I believe this game was the catalyst which sent us on our way. It was a game that could have made or broken Bob's Liverpool, but of course we won and grew in strength.

THE GAME STARTED well for us and we looked busy all over the pitch. I received an early pass from Hansen and had a nice early touch, felt settled and from then on just felt good about my game. I passed well and kept the ball moving quickly. Mostly forward to Ronnie, who was my wing partner. We'd always exchange passes and move, opening up the angles for a pass infield, looking to find Souey or Kenny.

Spurs, though, posed a threat. Early on, Archibald beat me for pace and I thought, "Bloody hell, this guy's alright". If someone was going to beat me for pace, I knew they had to be quick. If someone was going to get the better of me, I knew they had to be decent. "I'll remember that for next time."

Or at least I thought I would. Soon Archibald had outfoxed Lawro and sneaked in behind the back four before slipping the ball under Bruce. We didn't deserve it, but it just underlined how dangerous the London team were. We were devastated. They were on top, had a lot of good possession and our fans must have wondered if we could do anything about it.

Ronnie Whelan saw a header flash wide and we began to get our passing going, but it was hard to break Spurs down. I felt that Ardiles, who could hurt you going forward, was having to sit back more and more and that suited us defenders. Rush had a first glimpse of goal after good work from Sammy Lee and Kenny, but he seemed to hurry his chance. This was Rushie's first game for Liverpool at Wembley and it was understandable if the early phase of the game had got to him.

It was the unexpected frame of Sammy Lee that came closest for us in that half when he swooped to header a neat chip from Kenny, unfortunately for Sammy and us, Ray Clemence was on hand to save it. It was odd to be playing against Clem at Wembley when for so long he had been our own, brilliant last line of defence. He was such a popular figure in both the dressing room and on the terraces. I remember a couple of months after Wembley, Schnozzle (Clem's nickname due to his huge beaky nose) returned to Anfield for a league game and got one of the best receptions from the Kop that I'd ever seen.

Today though, he was proving a thorn in our side and the frustration continued when efforts from both Souness and Lawrenson zipped wide. We had to make that long walk back to the dressing room, pleased that we'd begun to get a grip on the game, but disappointed to be a goal down. Personally I was really pleased with my own game. I had been passing crisply and tackling cleanly. I had been hungry to get forward and felt I was supporting Ronnie really well.

In the dressing room the boss and the staff were disappointed that we were losing and gave out some bollockings, but no one said anything to me so I must have been doing reasonably well. It was Ronnie Moran who dished out most of those ticking-offs. You could always hear Ronnie's voice, wherever we played. Even at Wembley when you're so far away from the managers, Ronnie's orders remained audible. If you weren't pulling your weight, you soon knew about it.

WE CAME OUT and began to put some good stuff together and again we had plenty of the ball. The problem was, when you played a team like Spurs, as a full-back you couldn't go charging down the wing attacking at will because they had players who would punish you. Garth Crooks and Tony Galvin had threatened our goal on the break and their ability was always in the back of my mind.

Bob was aware of how good they were too and had warned us defenders to be cautious. The manager was a secret fan of Glenn Hoddle. He was a wonderful player, but I don't think he would have ever played for Liverpool as he was not a team player and you couldn't guarantee that he would perform week in and week out. That notion was perhaps a little unfair.

I would have loved to have seen him at Anfield because he was such a skilful guy and probably far more naturally creative than the midfielders we had. That's not a put down to Terry McDermott or Souness. Glenn had some fantastic skill, but the question was could he produce it every week? It was a question that blighted Glenn's' career and hampered his England chances. Bob was the same as those England managers that didn't regularly select Hoddle, he wanted consistency and he got it from Souey, Ray Kennedy and Jimmy Case.

Spurs also had Tony Galvin, who was a tricky and quick winger. He picked up a knock early on, but still caused us problems. Mickey Hazard was a brilliantly talented young midfielder and Ossie Ardiles had been a revelation since his move to England in 1978. His compatriot, Ricky Villa got on in the second half and, whilst he wasn't as consistent as Ossie, he had shown with that wonder goal on this very ground in the previous season's cup final just how good a player he could be.

That's what we were facing and we had another reason to be wary early on in the second half when Bruce saved smartly from a Mickey Hazard drive. At 1-0, though, we knew we were well in it and as the half went on we had more and more of the ball. My own game continued to thrive on the occasion. I remember one moment when I thought to myself that this truly was my day.

I had been beaten by a one-two and Steve Perryman was put in and galloping forward. I thought to myself, "We're in danger here" and went full pelt to try and retrieve the ball. I remember I came sliding in just as he was about to cross it and made the tackle, taking it off his toe. That felt good. Now all we needed was an equaliser. I thought to myself, "I do not want to lose here, I'm playing too well to lose this match, Come on!"

McDermott and Kenny both went close, but again Clem was equal to their efforts. It can be frustrating. We were all playing well, seeing a lot of the ball, but we couldn't get that clear sight of goal that we needed. It went on and on and we struggled to break them down. I'm thinking, "We are never going to score here, I know it. It's going to be one of those days." We'd played so well. I'd played so well.

We wouldn't stop though. We never gave up. And we were lucky enough to have players who could come up with a flash of brilliance. Kenny, Souey, you'd expect them to do something, but today our match-winner would be a youngster playing his first game at Wembley. Ronnie Whelan never lacked for confidence and with only three minutes left he was left unmarked as he hovered on the edge of the box and was in the right place to sweep a low centre from our substitute David Johnson into the bottom left hand corner.

We'd done it. We'd left it late, but we'd done it and from there we knew there would only be one winner. We didn't want another half an hour and so we pushed for a winner in normal time. Rushie almost got it for us, but Clemence, of all people, knew that against us you had to concentrate for the whole match. He saved and we faced extra time.

Spurs had had their chance and like a lot of teams discovered that to beat Liverpool you have to play hard for the entire 90 minutes. How many times did we score late goals? We always kept going and once we did score that late goal we always went on to win.

We all play today in the Masters football. We were two down recently to Sheffield Wednesday and came back in the last minute, made it 2-2 and won 3-2. You have to beat our Liverpool by playing for the whole game. We never gave it a thought that we could be beat. We hated losing and that attitude won us trophies. Occasionally people called us "lucky", but that was wrong. We just kept going. The last minute was the same as the first. We were winners.

WEMBLEY IS A sapping pitch to play on, but whenever we had extra time Bob made it clear that we weren't to sit down whilst he gave us his pep talk. Lawro had only been with us for nine months and he flopped to the ground. "Get up, son," said Bob.

"But I'm knackered."

"I don't care, get up."

It was a boiling day, but Bob knew that the Spurs players were going to see us all standing and think "Bloody hell, they're still fresh." It's an age old trick, but it works. Particularly if you've just equalised late on. The other team are on a downer. You've got to ram home every tiny advantage.

The club had this incredible winning attitude and it rubbed off on us players. It was the same with injuries. We didn't get injured because you knew if you complained about a slight knock you'd be treated like a leper. You were no good to anyone. They hated the treatment room. It was empty. No one dared go in there because you would be out.

The first half of extra time was cagey, but in the second period we began to open Spurs up and with nine minutes left we got our goal. Again it was Ronnie, doing what all good midfielders should, popping up in the box and getting goals. Kenny had perhaps looked offside when he received the ball, but the flag stayed down and he could take his time, pick his man and get in the cross. Once he'd stuck the ball past Clem, Ronnie was away. There was nothing wrong with his young legs and he sprinted away to greet our fans. They were so important to all of us. The fans aren't close to you at Wembley, but you could always hear our lot. Magnificent.

Spurs were beaten. Of course they had to come at us a bit, but you can murder teams on that big pitch when they're stretched and in the last minute, Rushie got our third after persistent work from Johnson. Our two new youngsters, playing their first games at Wembley for the club, had got our goals and that again underlined that this was the new Liverpool up to its old tricks. These guys had now got a taste of success and wanted more, much more. That's why it was such a significant victory.

Brucie, as well, was savouring his first medal and he began a tradition of coming up with something eccentric. We had said to him before, "If we win, you should do something different". I think he was racking his head during the game what he should do and so afterwards he starts walking his lap of honour on his hands. We were all in hysterics.

Bob must have been like, "What the fuck is he doing, man! He'll break his bloody wrists, man." But that was Bruce. You couldn't tell him what to do or what not to do. He'd never been part of anything like this. We got back to the dressing rooms and we were in the bath with the cups. It was great, despite winning European Cups, this felt as good. The club had taken this game so seriously, maybe even more so than the Paris match even. It was vital that this new young team learn how to win if the club was continue on its successful path. And boy did we go on to great success.

We left for Liverpool that night and had far too many beers on the train and a massive bun fight! I had been presented with the Man of the Match award. It had gone so well. Everything I did came off. I had tackled hard, but fair. I was quick, I was defending and attacking and it felt good. I got a £3,000 prize from the *Sun* newspaper and had to give £1,000 to charity (my wife's school in St Helens), £1,000 to Liverpool's youth development scheme and just kept a grand for myself. I only saw about £200 of that as the taxman got a nice chunk and I think I spent most of that on buns!

We returned to Liverpool and there was no ceremony. It wasn't that big a deal to anyone else. No one realised then what an important win it had been; how it would spawn so many more glorious and glamorous nights. We were back training hard on the Monday, it was a case of "put away your medals, and let's get on with it. There may be more then at end of the season, so let's work hard". That was another secret of ours. We forgot about success just as quickly as we forgot about defeat. That was the Liverpool way. Don't live in the past.

I had already been at Anfield for three-and-a-half years and it seems strange, but that season and that match made me feel like a real part of the team. That sounds funny because I scored the winner in the European final; but I had been dropped. I wouldn't be again until I left the club. There were many other games, but this one was significant to the club and to me. Without question, I believe that match was the basis for winning the European Cup again in Rome two years later.

We became unstoppable. Teams were apprehensive of us and even great players like Hoddle must have feared us. We would get on a roll and dominate the division and steamroller teams. We didn't look after ourselves at all, but something was right. We weren't told what to eat or anything. How we survived I'll never know, but we actually thrived on it. It was the best time of my life.

Bob Paisley's new young Liverpool side had our opponents on the back foot. Another great era was ahead of us.

It was Brian Clough who once said, "All you get at Liverpool is a cup of tea." He was right.

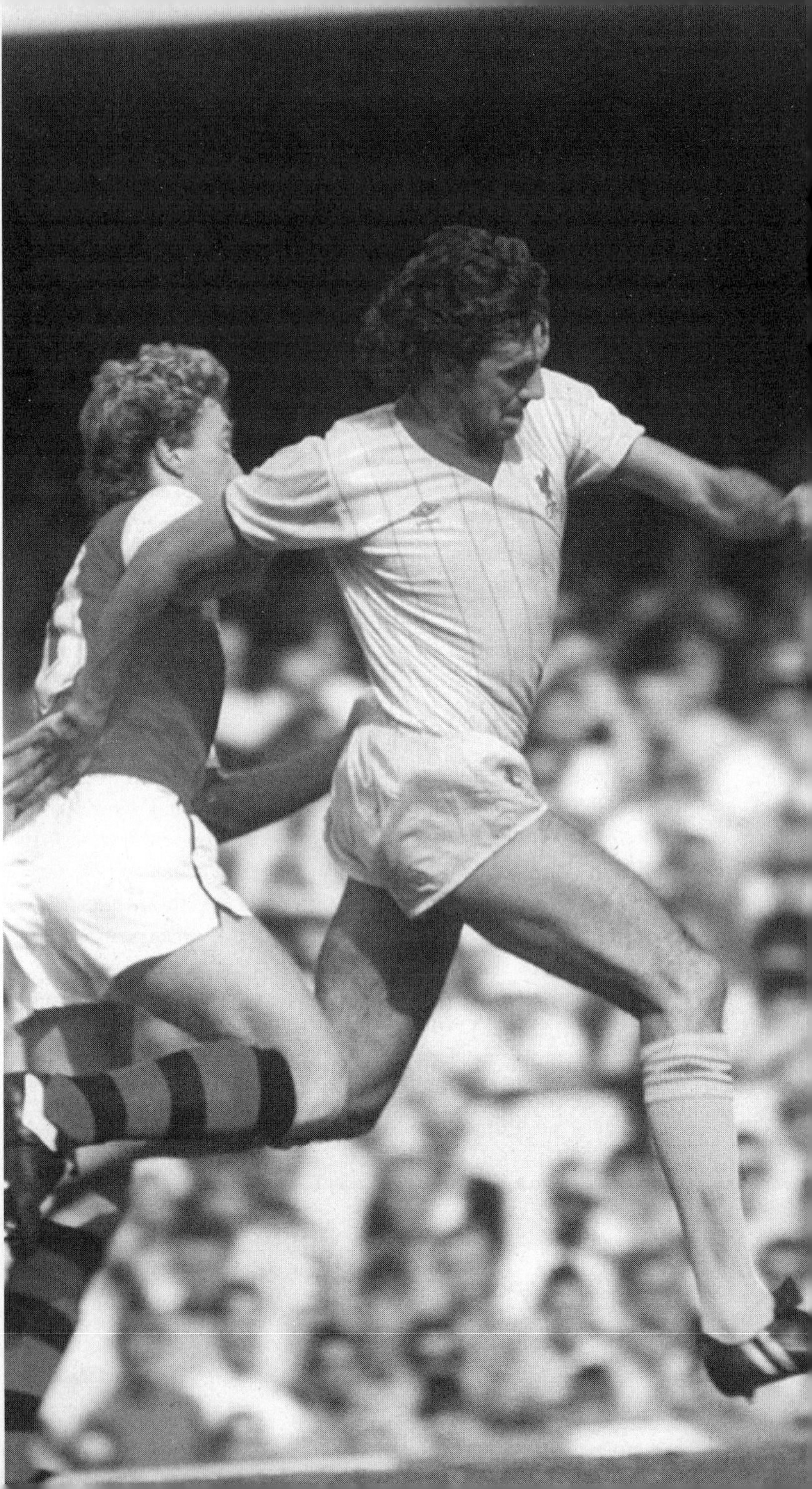

MARK LAWRENSON: BORN 2 JUNE 1957, PRESTON; 341 GAMES, 17 GOALS

Mark Lawrenson

Liverpool 1 AS Roma 1
(Liverpool won 4-2 on penalties)

European Cup Final

Wednesday 30 May 1984

"COME ON ALAN, come on son. Just stick this one away and we're European champions. Stick this away and let's go and have a beer, mate. Come on." Some of the lads couldn't bear to watch. They turned their backs or looked through the cracks of their fingers like children watching a horror film. I had to watch; after all it's always fun to see a mate make a tit of himself. We had reason to be nervous. The five planned penalty takers had been beaten by the youth team in a mock shoot-out before we left for Rome. Joe Fagan had watched horrified and said, "Bloody hell, we better win this in the allotted time." We hadn't and now we were going through the hell of a penalty shoot-out.

Alan Kennedy placed the ball on the spot. An army of photographers had de-camped behind the goal; their fingers primed to capture the moment that we hoped would make us Champions of Europe. Alan had missed his penalty in that shoot-out against the kids so we were all concerned. As he placed the ball though, he looked back at us and gave us the faintest of smiles. Maybe this *was* going to be OK. Just maybe.

It was like living in a slow motion replay. Alan ran up confidently and swept the ball low and into the net. There's a split second of nothing. Then; "Oh, my God. We've done it!" Then we're off and running towards our hero. It's bedlam, complete madness and we're champions of Europe.

It was the greatest of feelings, of course it was, but in a way, looking back it was almost logical that this team should win the

European Cup. We had been together as a group and grown together, first of all under Bob Paisley and then seamlessly under Joe Fagan.

WE'D JUST WON the Football League three years running. Do you know, I never even realised we'd done that. It sounds terribly blasé doesn't it? That's just how the club wanted it though. Any success was played down and you learnt not to dwell on what you'd achieved but to just get on with winning more. And that success was never glorified within the club. Never hyped up. As soon as we'd won something, that was past. History. We looked forward to winning the next trophy. We'd get our league winners' medals on the first day of pre-season. Ronnie Moran would walk in with a box-full of them and he'd look at you and say, "Did you play fourteen league games last season? Twelve? Oh, unlucky." It was so matter of fact. It sounds daft, but I only thought about the three titles on the spin from 1982 to 1984 a few years ago. Only then did I think about what an immense achievement it was. Strange, isn't it? But that's how we were.

I joined Liverpool late in the summer of 1981. When I first spoke to the club I didn't tell them that I had been sent off pre-season playing for Brighton and that I was going to be suspended for a few games. I thought if I said anything about it they wouldn't take me. You fear the worst and you are so keen to come to a club like Liverpool that you don't want to jeopardise it. Looking back it's silly, because maybe Bob would have liked the fact that I had a bit of the devil in me.

My first season was transitional. Not so much for me, but for quite a lot of the new players that Bob had brought in. I started my Liverpool career at left-back as Phil Thompson was still playing in the middle. When you were coming to the end of your career at Liverpool, you got an extra run in the team from August to Christmas. If you had done so well in your career, they kept with you, gave you a chance; and then came the cut-off point, "No, thanks. You've been great and on you go."

So certain players were having that last spell. It was all change really. Brucie had come in for Clem, Rushie was making his way into the fold, Ronnie came in, Craig Johnston and me. We started so badly that season and by January things had to change. The Boxing Day defeat at home to Manchester City was vital. A true turning point. Brucie made a couple of mistakes, the pitch was crap, but as a team we stunk. Joe Fagan blasted us after that match. I only witnessed that twice. "I've had enough of this, this is absolute crap, sort it out now!" It was strong stuff. Even the seasoned players like Souey and Dog's Bollocks - as Kenny Dalglish was affectionately known - were surprised by it. It shook us up. And Bob shook the team up.

WE WENT TO Swansea, managed by John Toshack, in the FA Cup and the gloom-mongers were all predicting that we were going out. Our form was crap and, to many, there was only one winner and it wasn't going to be us.

I was in the hotel lift the morning of the game with Bob. He was the master of the unfinished sentence and you had to try and interpret what he was saying. "Can you play on that one?" he said. "Can you play on that left-sided one?" Well, I had played left-back so I just said "Yeah". I didn't know what he actually meant and it turned out I was left side of midfield. We won 4-0 and I scored and the mood changed. The new players had taken their chance, this was the future and the old boys, who had achieved so much, were gone. Thanks, but so long.

The team just pushed on from that moment. We won the league from nowhere that year and by the time that Rome came around two-and-a-half years later we were at our peak. As I say, it was the logical next step that we should go on and win the top prize in Europe. Even if that was with a new manager.

When Bob retired in the summer of 1983 to become a club director and Joe Fagan became manager, it didn't seem like much of a change. Everybody loved Joe in the squad. The press had all been harking on about how Liverpool under Joe were going to struggle. How he could never follow Bob and how his lack of frontline managerial experience was going to cost the team. We came in for pre-season and Souey sat us down and just said, "Wouldn't it be fantastic to win a few things for this bloke?" Everybody to a man was with him and that showed. There was a steely determination that summer. Noone wanted to let Joe down. That's how we all felt about him. We all really loved him.

What was important was the continuation. Joe just kept doing the same things that had brought success under Paisley, just as Bob had provided continuity from Bill Shankly. Most importantly, the team hadn't changed. We had great players. Kenny and Rushie were feared all over Europe. Kenny was amazing. He was getting on by then (Dalglish turned 33 in March 1984), but his head never slowed down; much like Teddy Sheringham in the modern era, only even better. Kenny had a big arse, he couldn't run, he couldn't head, but what a player. Among the best of all-time.

THAT PARTICULAR SEASON was incredible. In 1983/84 the Fagan factor was the most crucial thing to our success, but we also knew each other so well, and it sounds daft, but we knew how bad we could be. Everyone outside the club thought that we were this machine, an unbeatable machine, but we knew that if we ever took our foot off the gas, we could be bloody awful.

Look at our match at Coventry in the December of that season. We were crap. Bloody terrible. We got beat 4-0 with little Terry Gibson helping himself to a hat-trick. We were awful. We did well to only let in four. I blame Hansen, always have for that one. He blames me, mind. We came in after that game and Joe just looked at the two of us. "Get changed." That was it. Monday, he called the team in for a meeting. "That won't happen again. Please tell me that won't happen again."

"No gaffer, that won't happen again."

"Good, let's go training."

It was similar in the FA Cup. We got beat 2-0 at Brighton. They seemed to have a hex over us at that time, but again we had been poor. Nothing much was said afterwards though. We drove up to London and stopped in a hotel in Marylebone. "Right, come on," said Joe. We followed him off the bus and into the bar. He bought us all a drink and said, "That's twice now, it's not happening again is it?"

"No boss." We had a couple of beers and kicked on to take the Championship and the Milk Cup. As much as we were awful on our off days, we only had those two all season. No other team could boast that kind of consistency.

AS FOR EUROPE, the club had built itself a history in the tournament and, whilst we were always desperate to add to the three European Cups that had been won, we never sat down as a squad or were told to go for it in one competition. We had done badly in Europe in the previous couple of seasons, but it wasn't an issue. It was just another tournament and so we got on with it. That was it.

Strangely the club progressed that year thanks to our fantastic form away from home. For so long, Liverpool's progress in Europe had gone hand in hand with incredible nights at Anfield. Not that season. In fact we often left ourselves with a lot to do after first legs at home, but we had enough about us to earn some great results on our travels.

The campaign began against the Danish Champions, Odense, but that's a game I remember very little about except that we won 6-0 on aggregate. The competition really got going in the second round when we were drawn against Athletic Bilbao, the champions of Spain.

That was tough. Bilbao were a really good side. They got a 0-0 draw at Anfield and were very physical. We knew it would be tricky, but took heart from the fact that the pitch out there was so close to the fans and it felt like an English game. They would have fancied themselves after drawing at our place and they hadn't made the mistake of building themselves up. Some teams get a draw somewhere like Anfield and that's it, they tell anyone who will listen they have won the tie, but not Bilbao. That made us think, "Christ, they must be a good outfit."

We played very well. Rush scored with a header and we were through. Rushie got the nickname Tosh after that. He didn't score many with his head, so we thought we'd liken him to the great John Toshack.

We always were confident of nicking a goal away from home. You had to be with Dog's Bollocks and Rushie up front. People didn't realise how good Rushie was away from home. He was our first defender. He'd have the full-backs not wanting the ball because he was on to them so quickly. He would look out of the corner of his eye and pretend not to be aware, but as soon as the keeper's arm came back he was off and on to the defender receiving the ball.

People go on about tactics today. We all do it. I work on the Television and get paid to do it, but back then, away from home, we had this great 4-5-1 formation and it was perfect. Kenny was a natural in that set-up and would just drop into midfield whenever we lost the ball.

OUR NEXT HURDLE was Benfica, the Portuguese Champions. Again we found it tough at Anfield, but again won through a Rush goal. We went to Portugal amid all sorts of predictions that we would be knocked out. I remember it was chucking it down that night and we arrived at the Stadium of Light very early.

The management were like, "Get out, go for a walk. We don't want to see you for a while. "We went out on to the pitch, an hour and three quarters before the game and the home section of terracing was chocker. It was packed, even in the rain. "These are a bit keen," I thought.

A lot has been made of the win at the Stadium of Light. It was a great victory. 4-1 away from home in Europe is always incredible, but their keeper had a 'mare. The first goal was crap; comedy. And it went on. Ronnie Whelan bagged a couple. After the first goal went in that was that. We had the away goal and both the crowd and the opposition were gone.

The first goal is vital in Europe. It always is. That was the only thing the management talked about when we went away from home. We were told to strangle a game and shut the crowd up. It was drilled into you. My first game for the club was a friendly at Athletico Madrid. It was Brucie's first big game in front of a full house. We were European champions and Bob Paisley said to all of us, "No antics, get on with the game."

Brucie had the home crowd behind him whistling and jeering and throwing oranges at him. Of course Brucie is throwing them back and joining in the fun. The crowd are loving it and the volume goes up with every little thing he does. Afterwards, Bob was incensed. "What the hell are you doing?"

"It was just a bit of fun, Boss," said Bruce.

"Don't do it. You don't need to antagonise or excite a crowd. You'll learn that in Europe you just get on with it quietly and shut the crowd up."

We'd learnt and now we were in the semi-final of the European Cup. Dinamo Bucharest were the opposition and they were a tough, organised team. Again we were at Anfield for the first leg and again it was tight. We won 1-0 thanks to a very rare headed goal from Sammy Lee, but the legacy of the game lay with just how angry Souey had made the Romanians. He had "allegedly" broken the jaw of one of their players and they were livid.

Dinamo were a good side to be fair to them, but they lost it because they just came to Anfield to defend. They had good strikers such as Sokol, who finished the season as the top scorer in the European Cup, but offered nothing. They man-marked Kenny, Souey and Rushie. They identified them as the key players and so, of course little Sammy Lee scored with a header. That Liverpool side had so many players who could find the back of the net. That season seven different players scored in our European Cup run.

We went out to Romania, it was in the old Eastern Bloc then, remember, and the atmosphere was scary. All cloak and dagger, intimidation and suspicion. And that was just at the airport. We're travelling to the stadium when these soldiers all ring the bus, looking for Souey. Here are these mean looking guys with shotguns and Kalashnikovs peering into the window trying to find the perpetrator and we've nowhere to hide.

It has been remarked upon that a few of us looked the same back then. I suppose a few of us did have the wavy hair and the obligatory 'tache. The soldiers are looking at each of us and we're like, "It's not me mate, try the fella at the back!" Eventually they found him and one soldier put his finger across his neck as if he was cutting his throat. Souey just shrugged his shoulders. He loved it.

It got worse. We went out to warm up and the ground was crammed full of hostile Romanians. Every time Souey touched the ball in that warm-up there were boos and whistles and jeers. So

Graeme of course was dummying the ball, playing keepy-uppy and sending the crowd berserk.

The game itself was even more hostile. They definitely tried to break his leg. No doubt about it. You should have seen his socks after the game. They were in shreds. He was brilliant that night. Brilliant. As was Rushie, who scored one wonderful goal, in fact he got both in a famous 2-1 win.

We were in the final. Joe came in and went quiet. He just stood there all solemn and we're like, "What have we done?" Just as we thought he was going to moan, he let out a massive "Yahooooo!"

England manager Bobby Robson had travelled out with us as the national side were soon to play Romania and he came into the dressing room saying that was the best performance from a club side away from home in Europe that he'd ever seen. Joe and Ronnie Moran were giving him daggers. They hated his praise. "Don't be silly Bobby, they weren't that good." As ever they wanted to knock us down a peg or two. Keep our feet on the floor. After all we hadn't won anything yet.

That win in Bucharest highlighted how mentally strong we were, because that is probably the most hostile of crowds you could wish to play against. We knew we had lots of good players, but, importantly, they had also seen it all. Even if we conceded a goal, there was no panic. Players didn't try and do things they couldn't. It was just a simple way of going about the game.

IT WAS A great team to play in because things were so simple. The back four was very settled, but people go on about how cool we all were and how we played flowing football from the back. That's wrong for starters. Whenever we got the ball back there we were told to look up and get it forward. To be fair, with Kenny around there was little else you could do. If he made a run and didn't get it, my God you got a bollocking. Hansen and me used to have some fantastic rows with Kenny about it. During the game there would be hell to pay.

Get it out of your feet and get the ball forward. But the important thing was accuracy. If you knocked it six inches wrong to Kenny, you got a blast. He was great at holding the ball up though. Rushie was different. He thrived on the long ball over the top and his pace was his main strength. If you played a bad ball to Rushie he would shrug his shoulders; but not Kenny, he would want to fight you. In the nicest way, of course.

We knew our strengths, and, as I said, we knew our weaknesses and so we didn't really care about whom we played in the final in Rome. Roma had played Dundee United in the other semi, but we probably knew more about the Italians. That was a great Dundee team, but we knew little about them at the time.

Anyway it was Roma who won through and we were to play them in their own massive stadium. We were nervously apprehensive. They were at home and you couldn't help but think they'd get more decisions at home; that's life. I never thought it was going to be a free flowing game. You didn't get flowing games against Italian teams back then, so you wondered that this might just hinge on a referee's decision and that was bad news for us. We needed a strong ref.

But rather than look at the situation negatively, we managed to convince ourselves that it was unhealthy for them to be at home and that turned into us realising just how much pressure they'd be under in front of their own fans. With all that in mind we flew to Rome feeling OK. The city, of course, held great memories for the club and its fans. Despite the memories, no one mentioned 1977. Phil Neal was still playing and the staff had all been there, but whilst they mentioned the legendary post-match party, there were no comparisons. This was a new team and there was no use banging on about the past.

WE ARRIVED IN Rome the day before the game, but we didn't train on the pitch. The buggers instead sent us to a local sports ground, and you wouldn't have let your dog crap on it. It was awful. It was in the middle of nowhere, it was just a park and Joe took one look at it, saw all the potholes and the divots and said, "Have a walk, get some fresh air and then we're off." Straight away we realised the authorities were at it. We'd be doing well to escape alive, let alone with the European Cup.

But the siege mentality can be a good thing, just ask Alex Ferguson, and after that we knew they were trying to fob us off. Bob had made sure we took our own chefs. They always employed two English chefs because if one came out of the kitchen, who was to say what would happen whilst he was gone? There was always one in the kitchen. You could say it was all quite paranoid, but I think on that occasion it was very necessary.

The week before the game, having finished our league programme, we had been in Israel for a training session and basically got on the beer. We trained hard and played the Israeli national team, beat them 4-1 and soaked up a bit of sun. We could relax, we knew how to do that, but we also knew when to get serious. When we came back and trained at Melwood on the Monday we looked and felt good. I was in earshot of Joe who turned round to Ronnie and said, "Christ, we're gonna have to hold these lot back. They're ready now."

We trained at Melwood on the Tuesday morning and then flew to Rome. There were one or two fans at Liverpool airport, but they were the ones who were at Melwood every day. The only way you knew it was a special game was there was more media attention, your missus goes on at you to get her a new dress and there's a bigger clamour for tickets.

On the actual day of the game, we woke up in the late afternoon, after a snooze. I was rooming with Phil Neal and we put the TV on and it cut to the stadium. It was threequarters full and that was four hours before the match. "Bloody hell, here we go," we thought.

That apprehension built into genuine excitement as we drove to the stadium. Rome in the spring is so beautiful and the stadium was like one of the Roman ruins with stunning statues all around. "Imagine playing here every week," I thought.

WE ARRIVED, AS ever, early and, while the kit was laid out, we were sent out on to the pitch. You had to climb down these stairs, so there we were in single file, walking out amid all the boos. Champagne Charlie (Souness' nickname) said, "Let's walk right around in front of them all. That'll shock 'em. " "Great, Graeme. Let's do that". So we did. They hated us for it, but it showed those fans that they didn't intimidate us. Souey was loving it, but it wasn't pleasant.

We started to walk back toward the dressing room. The boys who had come from Middlesbrough; Souey, Craig, David Hodgson had got us massively into Chris Rea. We loved him. Hodgy started singing that song, I Don't Know What It Is, But I Love It. We're going single file up the steps, past the opposing dressing room singing the lyrics to this song. I say lyrics. We knew about one line and kept repeating it at the top of our voices.

And I don't know what it is, but I love it

We were only footballers remember.

The Roma manager, Nils Liedholm, later said he was giving a team talk as we were going by singing and he thought, "Christ, we may struggle against this lot." Apparently the Roma players suddenly looked drained. They went white.

Not that we were as calm as we made out. You would get nervous for every game, but this wasn't just any old game, and so if you weren't nervous here, there was something wrong with you. There was never any of that banging fists on chests or shouting. That wasn't our style. People just did their own thing. I used to go into the treatment room and do the *Daily Telegraph* crossword, admittedly the small one. I wanted to be out of the way because everyone talks so much bollocks before a match. I was of the opinion that physically, the training would take care of you, but it was mentally that counted most. By quarter to three on a Saturday you had better be right.

I would switch off for that last hour or so before kick-off. As long as the boots and kit were on, then fine. Hansen would just sit and read the programme, Nicol would be ready, full kit on, the works, at a quarter to two. He would go into the bog with Kenny, sit in different cubicles and they'd do the quiz from the programme together.

Away from home was different because of whiling away the time on the overnight stay. We had a curfew so we were stuck in the hotel. I ended up looking for things to do. That night I just read. I picked up an Italian newspaper and just flicked through it. Looking at the pictures of course!

Joe said nothing special. He made the team-talk at lunchtime and just ran though some of their players. They had some top players who needed mentioning. Their midfielder and captain Nappi, the brilliant Brazilian Falcao, Cerezo. Graziani, Conti. All had played in the 1982 World Cup. Two, Conti and Graziani, had won the thing. As we walked out and prepared for kick-off the crowd went bonkers. The Liverpool fans were in a distant end and they looked lost amid the hordes of home fans, but soon we could hear their voices breaking through the din.

FALCAO ACTUALLY TRIED to score from the kick-off, but that just gave Bruce an early touch and us some much appreciated and needed early possession. We began to knock the ball about nicely, and our shape looked solid. Souey was sitting in front of Alan and myself and dictating the pace of the game as we set about trying to shut the crowd up.

I remember Ronnie Whelan cut Falcao in half early on. Souey was known for it, so if he'd done it he was going to get booked. Ronnie could do it and just give an innocent look. "Sorry Ref, I mistimed my tackle."

You want a good early touch, but mine wasn't. I played a dodgy ball to Phil Neal, who had to go in with an Italian and he fouled him. It was a shocking pass. He was booked, so my start wasn't very good. Soon though, I tackled their forward and caught the ball nicely. I thought that was good. My confidence was back and then we scored.

It was a mad, messy affair. A massive case of Rick O'Shea, the Irish striker! It hit the keeper's head, bounced about a bit and then Neal pounced on it and shoved it in. We were one up and we knew we had to keep playing. You couldn't sit on it. There was no point, not with Rushie in the team because he could always get you a goal. He was awesome that season. He scored 48 goals in all competitions; phenomenal. If that is such a major thing in your team's make-up, why give it up? Kenny dropped back in a bit to bolster numbers in midfield, but that's what he always did away from home. Kenny had broken his jaw that season and wasn't quite himself, but listen, a half-fit Kenny was better than what most clubs could offer and you could see that Roma were playing with one eye on him. Graeme actually netted straight away after the goal and the crowd went deathly silent, but the linesman had his flag up for offside.

Graziani brought a good save from Bruce and Roma were soon trying to get at Neal and Alan Kennedy down the wings. Perhaps they considered our full-backs as our ageing weak link, but that was to underestimate the two of them. The defence were having to work hard, but looked comfortable running up to half-time and we were confident of going in one up. Then the sucker punch.

Conti got the ball into the penalty area and it was Pruzzo who nipped in between Alan and myself and, to be fair, glanced a lovely header past Bruce into the top corner. Alan must have been picking his nose at the time. Pruzzo was definitely his man!

At half-time there was no panic. "Keep playing, keep passing". That was all we were told to do. We had managed to shut the crowd up once and would have to do it again. That was fine. Our run in the competition had been built on doing exactly that and we all felt we could do it again.

I had to make a timely interception early in the second half to stop Conti whilst Graziani had a similar header to Pruzzo, but this one fortunately flew into Bruce's arms; as did a snap shot from Falcao. These were half chances and to be honest the second half was quite dull. Both teams were very cagey and happy to keep possession.

We managed to slow the pace down and frustrate the Italians with Graeme keeping the ball, coming backwards if needs be and generally using our experience to nullify a game that could have become awkward had the home fans got their tails up.

We had one scare near the end when Brucie came for a cross and he dropped it. The ball sat up and luckily I headed it calmly back into his arms. He gave me a look that said, "Thank God you're here". It took a lot to frighten Bruce, but he looked terrified for that moment.

Extra time was the biggest of nothings. I thought they would come at us, but they didn't. We were the away team, why should we chase the game when Roma were reluctant to leave any gaps for Rushie to exploit.

It had been a long hard season, but you don't hear players going on about that. Training is a pain in the arse. You just want to play. If you are successful you are playing more games and training less and if you are winning games then your legs don't ache. The final was my 66th game of the season – I had missed only one in all four competitions – but you wouldn't have swapped that for anything. It meant you were doing well.

It also explained maybe why that extra time was played at such a snail's pace. It was walking football. We all kept our socks rolled up. If you let them down you would be bollocked by the bench. That and sitting down during an extra time break, they hated both. After extra time Joe came on and said, "As far as I'm concerned, you've done it. Away from home, you've done us proud."

SO TO PENALTIES. It's always the cruellest of ends, but we felt we already had some sort of moral victory and whilst we were desperate to win, Joe had shown by his words just how proud he was of us. He named the five takers and young Steve Nicol insisted on taking the first. He blazed it over. When you don't take one yourself you have to say unlucky. So I said, "Unlucky Nico... you dickhead!"

It's easy when you're watching, though, and I spent the time with Alan arguing who would take the tenth and eleventh penalties if it came to it. Here we were, these two supposedly cultured, composed centre-halves arguing about who would go last. Pathetic.

Neal scored his pen to level things and then came Bruce's famous wobbly legs. That was Bruce, always trying to steal the limelight. Brilliant. He had me in stitches. It certainly seemed to get to both Conti and Graziani. The two players who had won the World Cup had been outfoxed by Grobbelaar and with Rushie and Graeme putting their spot-kicks away it was all down to Alan Kennedy, who, of course, made no mistake.

We got the cup and our medals, had the pictures taken with all the staff and then we went down to the supporters. I did an interview with the ITV guys, but to be honest it's hard to recall much after that because it's all such a blur.

Later, when it sank in that we'd done it – we'd won the European Cup, it felt strange that it had been done via penalties. Liedholm, the Roma coach, said afterwards that he wished we could have had a replay at Anfield. Yeah right, all the best. We were the neutral team because we had to go to Rome and we had again proved how unfazed we were by it all.

THE PARTY WAS something else. The best I've ever been to. It was in what was like a mobster's villa on one of the Seven Hills of Rome. Crown Paints, our sponsors had organised this amazing venue. I can remember going in through the electric gates along this winding road that took you up to this incredible place.

The chief executive of Crown Paints stood up and said, "I'm not going to talk for long, only to say, anything you drink, anything, is down to us. Have fun!" Bloody hell, it must have cost them some money as we certainly did drink some.

We couldn't completely relax as we had a close-season tour to Swaziland in Africa to see to. We flew back from Rome on the Thursday and then went on the Friday to Swaziland where we had to play Tottenham over two weekends. The first game, half of us didn't play. Joe said we had a throat infection. Yeah, right. We were all still pissed. The party hadn't stopped. The hotel had a golf course and a casino, so it was all fun. I think we were all drunk for about a week! We didn't fancy playing much, but still managed to beat Spurs 5-2 and they'd been training.

It's a different era now, so our treble that season gets a little overlooked, especially as it was the Milk Cup and not the FA Cup we won, but that's to be expected. I look back on it and it makes me proud. It's a terrible thing to say though, but the whole thing was so businesslike. That was the way it was. The way the club ran. It was so without glitz that you didn't ever feel part of this massive thing; something that only one other club could claim to match in history.

I suppose we were though, weren't we?

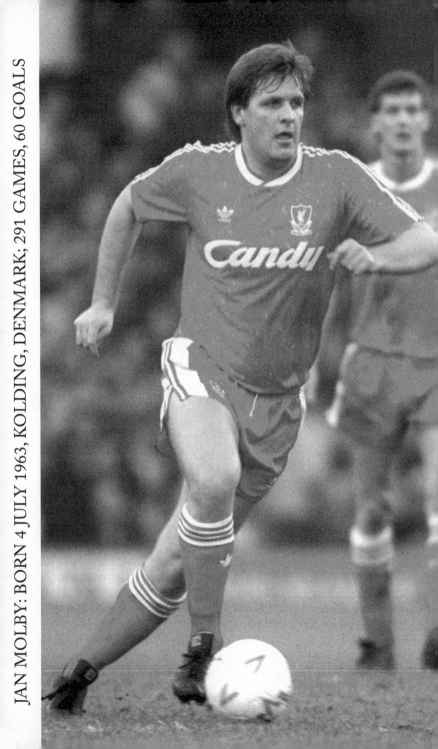

JAN MOLBY: BORN 4 JULY 1963, KOLDING, DENMARK; 291 GAMES, 60 GOALS

Jan Molby

Liverpool 3 Everton 1
FA Cup Final
Saturday 10 May 1986

ALL I WANTED was to get up those steps. All I wanted to do was get my medal. The first FA Cup final I had watched on television back in Denmark was in 1971 when Arsenal had beaten Liverpool to win the double. Now I was about to get my medal for Liverpool, a medal that meant that this great club had achieved that very same feat. Every year back home we'd all sit around the TV set and watch the final. Some of the games had been average, but who cared, you wanted to stay and watch the cup being given to the winning captain and the teams climbing those famous 39 steps.

I would sit there as a boy and wonder what it was like to walk up those stairs a winner. That must be amazing. Now here I was doing it. It lived up to and surpassed all the expectations that I had always had as a dreaming lad.

Despite a hard season, despite the hard match, that climb was the sweetest and easiest of my life. My first season at the club, mind you, was a far tougher ascent as I battled my way into both the team and the fans' hearts. Both were missing a certain Graeme Souness.

There was never any pressure from within the club. It was never brought up. They never specifically said, "We want you to replace Graeme Souness," that wasn't an issue. All they said was that they wanted a central-midfielder and I was the type they were looking at. They took me on a ten-day trial and at the end of that I got a two-year contract.

I flew in on a Sunday and trained with the first team all week. That was something. They had just won the European Cup, which I watched back home in Denmark understanding just what they had achieved. I had played for Ajax in that season's European campaign and so I knew how hard a trophy it was to win.

Liverpool was a massive club. It was *the* club. The best. And from outside of Anfield everyone was telling me just how much pressure I must be under. I'm the new guy; I've arrived here, in the eyes of the fans, to replace their hero, Graeme Souness. *And* I'm one of the first foreign players to have been bought by the club. In the press too, they would go on about it, but that's life, that's football.

No one at Liverpool cared about any of that rubbish. Joe Fagan did his best to keep that tension off my shoulders and that meant letting me sample life in the reserves. It was known that Liverpool, back then, would buy good young players and slowly let them learn the Liverpool way of doing things. I was ahead of the game as I started over 20 first team matches that season. In fact up to Christmas I played 19 games, but then I was in the reserves a lot, whilst getting a taste of the first team from the bench.

It was agreed wisdom at the club that you would give a new player between six and twelve months to settle and then they came good. They had so much faith in their own ability to spot a quality individual that it didn't worry them if a player wasn't shining in the first team. "Alright, he'll be OK, give him a few more months and it'll be fine." Chris Lawler ran the reserves by then and he would just pull me aside and say, "Don't worry, this is how it works at Liverpool."

If that was the everyday way of doing things, the 1984/85 season itself was far from the norm at Liverpool Football Club. We finished second in the league, were runners-up in the European Cup and reached the semi-final of the FA Cup. A good season? You'd have thought so, but not at Liverpool. We had won no silverware and that was unheard of. Coupled with that was the Heysel Stadium disaster which occurred at the European Cup Final. A terrible event which served to darken our thoughts about the campaign still further.

JOE RESIGNED AT the end of the season with Kenny, of course, getting the job as player-manager – a brave move by the board. We were as surprised as anyone. It wasn't an obvious choice as none of us felt he wanted to go into management and, who knows, if he hadn't been offered it then, he may have never become a manager.

Luckily he did and he became a great help to me. Pre-season can be very frustrating if you aren't playing 90 minutes. We couldn't go on a continental pre-season tour because of the aftermath of Heysel so we based ourselves down south in Brighton and played friendlies around the south-coast. We played a few and I was in and out, but Kenny made it clear to me that he liked the way I played and saw this as a big season for me. It made me feel good, this is the manager talking, but this is also Kenny Dalglish.

If I had Kenny making me feel good, Kenny had Bob Paisley. He was a presence at the club and an aid to Kenny. I was only aware of him as a past manager, but some of the lads enjoyed him being around. Bob helped, but so did Ronnie Moran, as he was the most experienced of the staff and he took a lot of the burden off Kenny's shoulders.

I had to get on with my own game. I had had my stint learning about the club and the country. Now was the time to deliver. Joe had played me in the Souness role in front of the defence, but Kenny saw that he could push me forward a bit more and have another fill in behind me. He chose Kevin MacDonald, who'd arrived from Leicester at the same time as me in 1984 and then also bought Steve McMahon from Aston Villa. Of course, when new signings like that arrive you are a little concerned about your place. When he signed Steve, many thought that was it for me, but Kenny pulled me aside and said, "Do you think Steve is here to replace you?"

"I don't know, Boss."

"Not in a million years. He's here to play with you."

When you think of a midfield player who plays off the front two you wouldn't picture me would you? You think of a dribbler, a quick player, someone who would pop up and score goals. I was none of those things. I was much bigger, much slower, but it suited me as I had much less defensive responsibilities and I could use the ball how I liked.

The club were great at realising how to maximise the strengths of their players. The team too. No one was ever jealous of anyone else. The team spirit was excellent. At Ajax for example if a new midfield player turned up, the other boys in midfield would have been the last ones to talk to him. Not here, they got on with it and if a new player arrived everyone would just hope that it was going to strengthen the team. That was so refreshing.

That made a change from my previous club, but what both set-ups had in common was the way in which they wanted to play football. Both clubs wanted to dominate and so both attacked. No game we ever played was viewed negatively or in a way that might stop the other team winning. It was all about us and our strengths.

I STARTED THE 1985/86 season OK, but wasn't exactly setting the world alight. Then we played Manchester United in the Milk Cup and my life at the club changed in one sweet evening. United had started the season in fine form. They won their first ten league games and under Ron Atkinson it seemed like their wait for a championship might just be over. It looked like their time had come as they led us by a goal to nil at Anfield, but then I managed to score two brilliant goals in front of the Kop.

I had scored a couple already that season, but with respect, they had been against the likes of Luton and Spurs. That's all very good but I'm sure there have been many players over the years who haven't truly made it at Liverpool, but managed to score against lesser teams. No, if you want to get noticed dribble past a few Manchester United players and slam the ball into the top corner from 20 yards. Unfortunately the TV cameras were on strike so my wonder goals weren't recorded, but years later Ron Atkinson gave me a video from someone who had a home camera in the ground. It's grainy, but you can see them. That was a turning point for me.

The fans certainly thought so. They had been slow to take to me and I understood that. Souness had gone and the team didn't win things. That second season, though, they realised I had something about me. Soon they were singing and calling me "Rambo" and you couldn't help but feel lifted by that support.

The dressing room had been a different matter. I settled there from day one. There's always one or two, but that 's life. The likes of Alan Hansen and Mark Lawrenson were a couple I didn't immediately take to, but they were senior and I think their policy was to have a little look at the new boy; "let's let him prove himself". It wasn't nasty or negative, it was just their way.

The rest, though, were great. Bruce Grobbelaar, Ian Rush, they were marvellous. Rushie and I hit it off. I was single, Rushie was semi-single and so we had time on our hands.

I was settling into life in my new home and I guess picking up the accent so soon adhered me to the fans even more. I spoke English OK, but hearing the Liverpudlian twang was a shock to the system. A lot of Scandinavians don't have an accent so I arrived speaking the Queen's Danish, so wherever I ended up I was bound to pick up that dialect and Scouse it was.

Jesper Olsen and I were on *Grandstand* before a United-Liverpool game, just months after I had arrived. I sounded like I had been living in Liverpool all my life, I still do I suppose. If you listen closely to Schmeichel he has a slight Mancunian twang and Brian Laudrup speaks English like a Glaswegian. There's no escape.

FEELING PART OF my new team and of my new city, I could start to think about winning the honours I had come here to win. The FA Cup was special to me after my youthful dreaming, but the club hadn't won it for 12 years. We were due a trip to the final, but that was a world away when Norwich City arrived at Anfield in the driving January snow.

The game was won with an orange ball, but that wasn't the only oddity. We played three at the back with me at centre-half. Kenny did that now and then, but never at home and certainly not against a Second Division team. Anyway we played well and won 5-0.

The next round we were at Chelsea and again we played with three at the back. That was tough, that was a proper hard game and maybe we were a bit fortunate to go through 2-1. Lawro got the winner.

Next was Third Division York City. We knew them as we had played them the season before. Anyone who thought it would be easy was wrong. They were tough opponents and boasted the likes of Marco Gabbiadini and John MacPhail in their side. In fact Keith Houchen, who would find fame with his diving header for Coventry in the following season's cup final, couldn't even get in their team. We knew it would be hard at their small little ground and the pitch was frozen. There was hay all over it and we had to put on the old all-weather astro trainers. They went one up and the place goes mad, but luckily we got a penalty straight away, which I scored, and we took them back to Anfield. It was a dubious penalty that one. No matter, we were always told, "If you don't lose, you're still in the cup."

In the replay York took us by surprise and we didn't play well. After 90 minutes it was 1-1 and a lot would argue that they should have won it as they scored a goal that was disallowed. In extra time I made it 2-1 and I think Kenny got a third. That was a tough night.

Watford in the quarter-final was again bloody hard. They came to Anfield and set their stall out and earned a 0-0 draw. It was a typical cup-tie, but as usual after the game there was no panic; we were still in the cup.

We went down to Vicarage Road, which was always a hard place to play. The pitch was knee high in mud, which made life difficult, and soon they were making things harder for us. They got themselves a free kick and with Barnsey about they were always going to have a chance. He curled in a beauty and we had to chase the game on the mud. Four minutes were left when Rushie did what he did best and chased a loose ball. Even on the mud he managed to get there a fraction before Tony Coton in goal and got brought down, penalty. Whilst there was no dispute about the decision, we had a few concerns about who would take the thing. I had missed a couple that season and before the first game at Anfield Kenny had handed the mantle of taker over to John Wark. In the replay, though, Wark wasn't playing and so Kenny turned to me and said, "D,you fancy it?" You don't say "No" and so I put the ball on the spot.

I took a lot of penalties for Liverpool and that was the only one when I felt "I really need to score this". I got one against Auxerre in the UEFA Cup years later that was a similar situation and I knew here that if I missed we're out of the cup. I took extra care. If the keeper doesn't move I would put it to his right. This time Coton just stood up straight and so I put it the other way. Rushie got the winner in extra time.

THE SEMI WAS a dull affair, but a tough game against a good Southampton team. Rushie was the main man that day and thanks to his two goals in extra time we were in the final. We came in and heard that Everton would be our opponents at Wembley as they had beaten Sheffield Wednesday and that just added to the excitement.

That was early April and, to be honest, we still thought we would only finish second in the league behind Everton and were all grateful for the chance to put things right at Wembley. Our league form, though, had started to pick up and I think that was down to the cup run and one important individual ingredient. Kenny Dalglish.

Kenny put himself back in the team in March and his presence was incredible, not only for us, but I think it made the opposition wary. Liverpool with Kenny will play a different way and I think teams backed off and that gave us a bit more room. He would drop off Rushie to receive the ball and create space to play and that helped us. We were winning by five and six regularly. We continued to put a run together and were really going some. The last 12 games were incredible.

We knew we'd be facing Everton in the final and now we were challenging them for the title too. It was so neck and neck between us. They had been favourites to win both only a few weeks before and had beaten us at Anfield. Bruce threw one in and Lineker got one that was five yards offside. It's never easy to let defeat in a derby game go!

AFTER THAT GAME, I believe Kenny and Alan went for dinner and philosophically suggested that this Liverpool team were the poorest they'd been involved in. I always found that unfair because we still had Bruce, Alan, Lawro, Nicol, Whelan, Johnston, McMahon, Rush. These were some of the best players the club has seen and they were in their prime, so those comments never rang true with me. They did serve to motivate me to up my game and my commitment to new levels. And maybe that's what they were gently prodding us to do.

After that match, though, the expectation on us was lifted and we seemed to play with more ease and I think Everton struggled with the pressure that was now on them not to blow their lead. They lost a match at Oxford and we were back in pole position and put together a run of ten wins and a draw in 11 games to sit on the verge of winning the title back from across Stanley Park. We just needed a win on the final Saturday of the season at Chelsea to clinch the title.

We trained on the Friday morning at Melwood, but disaster struck as I had a tummy bug. Really nasty. You know what I mean. I travelled to London despite saying I felt sick to my stomach. I was on the bus and I felt like death. They wanted me there just in case. I got to London, but there was no chance I was going to be involved.

We won 1-0 to wrap up the title thanks to Kenny's volley and I'm watching and, although I'm ecstatic, I thought "I'm going to miss the final here." Lawro stepped in for me in midfield and did well and I was thinking; "They're not going to give him only one game, this is Mark Lawrenson we're talking about here. An exceptional footballer."

I was very edgy. It had been a wonderful end to the season, but now, because of a silly bug it looked as if I might miss the finale. The celebrations after the win at Stamford Bridge were muted, but after championship wins, they often were. For some of the boys it was their sixth or seventh title and this season it was different as we had the opportunity to achieve something no Liverpool team had done previously. We wanted the double.

One man who *was* ecstatic was our often-ignored midfielder Kevin MacDonald. He did his job very well. He was simple and he was at the right club to have those qualities utilised. He got on with his job and that helped the team. He was competitive and he always gave all he had. Because of that I could get on and play my attacking game. If we were one down he wasn't going to get us back in it, but when it came to helping us play and find a rhythm, he was great.

I hoped so much that I would be in there with Kevin come the following Saturday. Lawro had done well, he always did, but I hoped that my progress and form over the season would stand me in good stead. I was there to pass the ball. I have been compared to Xabi Alonso today and that is very nice.

I was fortunate because I always played the game with my head up and could see things around the pitch. That's not big headed, that's just how I had grown up. When you watch in the stands there is always a pass that everyone sees and then there is one that people don't see. That's usually the one that can open a defence up and that is what I managed to do. I had that ability and that vision.

I sat and worried about my place in the team whilst the city of Liverpool came alive with cup final fever. It was electric. I lived on the house on the Wirral next to a school. As far as I was concerned normally the school might as well have not been there. It was so quiet and the kids were so well behaved. Not that week. It would start at a quarter to eight and, if you're a young footballer, at a quarter to eight you're asleep. Every morning the singing would start, the kids would be knocking on the door. "Come on Jan, lad. Beat Everton, Jan." Everybody was talking about one thing and one thing only, the cup final.

I couldn't blame them. This was all new to me too and I was as excited as any punter or school kid. It was special. OK, so the league was celebrated quietly, but this was exciting. Liverpool had recently won the European Cup, but not one of our squad had ever played in an FA Cup final, not even Kenny, so this was one to get a buzz from. It was a big, big game.

There was a lot of interest and for me, I knew that was not only confined to Merseyside. The Danish squad had met up a week before to prepare for the World Cup that summer in Mexico. I knew they would all be watching. I would have loved to have been the first Dane to play in the Cup final, but Jesper Olsen had played for United the year before. It was a big thing, you grew up watching the English Cup final and now here I was, getting the suit fitted and recording a crap song.

WE TRAVELLED DOWN on the Thursday and stayed at a hotel near Watford. We trained on the Friday morning but had no indication about what team Kenny would pick, but we never did. We relaxed on the Friday evening, had the usual pool competition that night before getting our heads down. I never had any problems sleeping, but in the back of my mind I was wondering if I would play or not.

I had been in the squad the previous May before the European Cup final, but missed out. It wasn't a heavy blow back then because I had been on the bench for most of the season anyway. This time though I felt that I had played 58 times and if I'm left out I've got to be unhappy, haven't I? I felt I had a reasonable chance, but at the back of my mind I knew they had won the league the previous week without me.

Soon though, fate took over. Gary Gillespie woke up on the Saturday morning with the same bug as I had and was out. You had to feel for him. That marked Kenny's hand and Mark went back to centre-half and I came into midfield. Would I have played if Gary had been fit? Who knows? To this day Kenny says he'll never tell me, not ever. I have a sneaky suspicion that I would have though.

Poor Gary. He had done so well and found it hard over the years to break up Mark and Alan's partnership and here's his chance and he gets ill. If he blames me for that bug, he's never let on, but if it helps; "I'm sorry, Gary."

At the time, though, you have to concentrate on yourself and as we left for Wembley, none of us knew the team. I've driven to games in World Cups, but nothing ever matched that journey. It was a sea of red and blue and where else has somewhere like Wembley Way on Cup final day? Brilliant.

Kenny waited until 15 minutes before kick off to tell us his team; a full half hour after he'd handed the teamsheet in to the referee. He sat us down and named it and that was that. No ceremony. I heard my name and I was sitting upright and ready to go. It's a tense time in that dressing room, but you get used to your team-mates' little quirks.

In the dressing room Brucie had this habit of kicking a ball at the wall until he turned off the light switch. That could be annoying. There were times when he'd hit the thing in the first couple of minutes and then it was a bit of fun, but there were times when it would take 15, 20 minutes. You'd be like, "Could you stop that, Bruce?"

"Oh, no," he'd say, "I've got to do it."

He did it early that day, thank God. I would just try to rest on the bench with a towel under my head. Not focusing or anything, just resting and clearing my head.

Next was Kenny's team talk. He simply said, "Let's not spoil all the good stuff we've done over the last three months. We've played brilliantly, won games comfortably, but this now is our biggest test. These are as good a team as you're going to play, it's going to be difficult, but don't panic, this doesn't have to be won in the first half." He was right again wasn't he?

I HAD A tradition of going out last which made it weird because I could hear the roar as Kenny and Howard Kendall emerged, but I was still all the way back. I'd been to Wembley before and won with Denmark, but this was different, this was jam-packed, electric, the best I've ever experienced. We later found out that fans had got n any way they could including clambering up the drainpipes and being hauled in through the toilet windows. Scousers can't bear to miss their team's glory days and for both sets of fans this was just about the biggest day yet. To win the FA Cup would always be fantastic, but to beat your greatest rivals in the final… it doesn't get any better than that.

I went back in 1988 to face Wimbledon, but we were expected to win, in 1989 it was strange because of Hillsborough and we were expected to win again; in 1992 it was quite flat because we were such firm favourites, but in 1986 every person in that ground truly believed their team was going to win and that made it incredible.

We were focused on the game, you don't want to get drawn into the occasion and once the whistle goes you have to be straight at it. For all you know it could be the last time you play at Wembley and you want to do so well, but you must not let it overawe you.

The hard sell was over, the excitement put to the back of our minds and the whistle blew. Typically, the game itself was going to struggle to live up to the pre-match hype and what we had on our hands was your usual derby. It was a scrappy start. It would, of course, open up, but the early exchanges were rough and disjointed.

Everton, though, desperate to right the wrong of us winning the title, and them losing the previous season's cup final to Manchester

United, settled the quicker. Early on they had a legitimate penalty shout waved away after Steve Nicol had tangled with Graeme Sharp. It was just a little nudge, but on another day it could have been given. Not today though.

Any game against that Everton team was a struggle. They played some great stuff, but they could compete for as long as it took. The two in midfield, Peter Reid and Paul Bracewell were particularly competitive and I have many memories of run-ins with those two.

Even if they weren't playing well they would be around you, kicking you. Reidy especially. He was a talker, always in your ear. "I'm here, Jan. I'm here." He was always at it. I loved playing against Reid and Bracewell. I had some tough games against them, my ankles can testify to that, but what a great midfield combination they were.

After 27 minutes it was Reid - who proved there was more to him than just brawn - that played a sublime pass over the top to Lineker and with Alan and Lawro left in his wake, he scored, despite Bruce's best efforts.

I never felt, "Oh bloody hell, we're 1-0 down in the Cup final." We were disappointed, but to be honest that was more with the way we were playing. We couldn't get going. In a way that kept our spirits up, because, yeah, we're losing, but we haven't started playing yet. We'd seen what they had, they were only one up, but that was a lucky goal and so we had to start playing.

We hadn't created much and we looked incoherent, but we thought to ourselves; "We can't play badly for 90 minutes; that happens sometimes, but surely not today." It may have been nerves, I don't know, but we were kicking too many balls just into the channels rather than playing to feet. We didn't have enough possession in that first half; we couldn't work the ball around and frustrate Everton.

On that big pitch we should have had that freedom. I fancied myself there, but then everyone did. Craig Johnston was always so confident and hoped his pace would work, Rushie would have hoped that his darting runs and pace would get him behind the back four and, of course, I hoped that I would be able to pass the ball all over the place. For over 45 minutes none of that was happening.

Everton have to take a lot of credit as well though. Trevor Steven, Kevin Sheedy, they completed that brilliant midfield, whilst the two centre-halves Kevin Ratcliffe and Derek Mountfield were well on top and winning everything.

WITH ALL THAT in mind, it was a despondent Liverpool dressing room at half-time. With Kenny playing, it was Ronnie Moran that gave the team talk. "This is not the Liverpool team I've been watching for the past three months. I know and you know that you're better, now go out there and play and enjoy it. You have nothing to lose and you'll win this game." He must have said that 50 times, "You'll win this game." By then end you had to believe him.

The thing was we started the second half even worse than we ended the first. In fact it became shambolic. They were on top, our passes were going nowhere, Brucie threw one right off the pitch and then he and Jim Beglin started at each other in our penalty area. Bruce felt he had let Jim know he was coming to claim a through ball on the edge of the area and that Jim hadn't got out the way. They barked at each other, but that was typical Bruce; he'd soon just get on with things as normal. That was our low point though. Ronnie Moran must have been spitting. Enjoy it? How could we?

The Everton players must have looked at it and thought; "This is done, we've won this." Maybe that's why they lost a bit of concentration. Gary Stevens was a good player, an England player and usually he would have cleared the ball downfield, but instead his mishit pass sloppily found Ronnie Whelan who put me in and at last we've caught Everton square at the back. I knew this was a chance to hurt them but my pass had to be right. There wasn't much space between the back four and the keeper so I had to put the right weight on it. Rushie made his run and the pass drew Bobby Mimms from his goal who felt he could get there. Rushie gets there first, goes around him and knocks the ball into an empty net. One each. We're back.

This is it now; we're going to win this. All the preparation, all the build-up, all the nerves, all the tension, they disappeared. We had a game of football to win and the shackles were off.

We had a scare, though, when Sharp's header looked in, but Brucie was too much of an athlete to let that go by him. It was a great save and the whole thing with Jim was clearly out of his head. In fact it was never mentioned again. These things always happen; mind you they're usually in training and not at Wembley during the FA Cup Final. They didn't have to apologise to each other though.

We were all new men. We were finding more rhythm and just after the hour I got the ball and burst into the box. I made my way to the byline and waited for Gary Stevens to make the challenge knowing that when he stretched I could knock the ball through his open legs. I delayed the pass and sent it across and then anything can happen. It was the first time in the match that anyone had attacked the byline and caused that sort of danger.

Kenny tried a flick, but the ball ran to Craig at the far post who slammed it into the goal. He was away. I chased after him, but all I could hear was, "I've done it, I've done it!"

He was desperate to score. He had tried to nick Rushie's equaliser, in fact he tried to nick everything, he tried to nick the FA Cup later I think. That was so special to Craig. He knew they'd all be watching back home in Australia. He drank in every moment of that celebration.

EVERTON HAD TO gamble, Adrian Heath came on, Gary Stevens went off, Sheedy played deeper and with that they had lost their potency. Their strengths were as a tight 4-4-2 unit and now that was gone and we found more and more space.

Just afterwards I should have put the game beyond doubt. I got the ball on the edge of the box and the Everton defence thought I would pass it to Rushie and so stepped up to catch him offside. I've seen the gap and taken it to the left and suddenly I'm in. Bobby Mimms came out and I've gone for a blaster around his feet and he blocked it. If I had only side-footed it, it would have gone in, no problem. That still bugs me to be honest. I mean it was a great day, one of my best ever, but I should have scored. And it would have clinched the game even more importantly.

Soon, though, we did. With six minutes left we had seven or eight players around our penalty box. We were defending deep and

Everton were coming on, but bang, bang, bang, we're 3-1 up. There was some great interchange in that move. Craig and Kenny knocked the ball to each other in our half and by doing so we had shifted their players to one side of the pitch. When I received the ball the right side of the pitch was empty and I knew instinctively that the ball had to go there. It had to go that way to allow Kenny, Rushie and Craig to come back into the equation and Ronnie Whelan was in acres. Ronnie was given the time to put it on his right foot and sit it up to Rushie, who banged it home.

After that we kept hold of the ball, knocked it about and enjoyed the end. Rushie should have got a hat-trick, but went to chip Mimms instead of lacing it. Who am I to talk though? You enjoy those last moments. We had worked so hard all season, but now we could have some fun. We'd earned that.

Reid was quiet by then. We wouldn't say anything either, there was too much respect between the players to rub it in. They knew they'd lost the football match and we just got on with playing down the clock.

THE WHISTLE WENT and it was pure joy and relief. Kenny ran to me and we embraced. Sometimes you wonder how much to celebrate especially at Liverpool, but this was unexpected. We had made history; we had won the elusive double.

We stayed in a hotel in the West End. The party was for wives, girlfriends, backroom staff and us players only. We had dinner and the players were looking to hit the town about midnight.

That night, though, I didn't fancy going out. Usually I would, but for some reason I wanted to get up to my room and watch *Match of the Day*. I never usually had an urge to get videos of my games or to watch *Match of the Day*, but that night I really wanted to. It had meant that much. I wanted to confirm what I thought had happened just had.

I was on my hotel bed with my two medals, League Championship and FA Cup, and a big cigar, which were always provided by Brucie. It had become a tradition. He had a big box of different cigars and you could take your pick. But then a couple of mates from back home knocked on my door and said, "What are you doing?"

"I'm quite happy to smoke this and watch the Cup final," I replied.

"No, not tonight you aren't. You're coming out with us to Stringfellows."

So, I got dressed. We arrived and there was a massive great queue and I'm thinking "How are we going to get in here?" The next thing I know the FA Cup has arrived on the outside with two of the minders and a couple of the lads. Thank God, I probably would have queued all night and then got a knock back. "You don't look like a footballer," they would have said. "You're too fat." Anyway we got straight in and sat upstairs drinking champagne with the FA Cup at my side all night. I reckon I felt as proud as Steven Gerrard did when he lifted the European Cup in Istanbul. He slept with it that night. I partied with the FA Cup as my way of celebrating.

That day, that match, that night, it was the pinnacle. The medals are there today and have pride of place in my home. Everyone wants to see them and I look back on that team and that time with great affection. We are still the only Liverpool side to win the double and that means a lot.

Poorest Liverpool team that Kenny and Alan had ever been involved with? I don't think so.

JOHN BARNES: BORN 7 NOVEMBER 1963, KINGSTON, JAMAICA; 409 GAMES, 108 GOALS

John Barnes

Liverpool 5 Nottingham Forest 0

League Division One

Wednesday 13 April 1988

I WOULD GUESS that the majority, if not all of the games chosen by the lads for this book revolve around the winning of trophies; be they FA, European or League Cups and I could have gone for the day we beat Everton 3-2 in the 1989 Cup final. The thing is, I prefer to look at a game and judge our performance. The night we beat Nottingham Forest 5-0 at Anfield in 1988 stands out because it was such a comprehensive performance against a top quality side. Nothing to do with trophies, or silverware, or championships, this was about us as a team and how brilliant we could be.

Forest came to us that night as wounded animals, spoiling to show just how good they were, how they could tame us. The game had been rearranged to midweek as we'd played and beaten Forest in the FA Cup semi-final just four days earlier to deny Cloughie a place at Wembley in a competition he was fated never to win. They were desperate for revenge. They had great players, internationals, they were considered the finest passing team in the country by many, but we played them off the park. I have looked at modern games and I have seen Arsenal completely outplay teams, but for ten minutes Henry would go off the boil or the team would slow down. I have not seen a performance where a team has dominated for 90 minutes like we did on that special evening.

That one night captured all that was great about our team. Movement, pace, flair, strength, it was all on show that season and 1987/88 is one that I recall fondly, a season where everything seemed to come off. I loved every minute of it.

MIND YOU, SIGNING for Liverpool in the summer preceding that campaign wasn't as smooth as some of the stuff we played against Forest and I remember many fans thought my heart wasn't in signing for their great club. There were whispers about Arsenal being keen on me, but that's all they were, whispers. I had lived in London for a number of years and so that did appeal to me, I won't lie. Having lived down there for so long I, like many Londoners, had preconceptions about life up north. What happened, though, was that Liverpool showed the most interest and what an option for a young footballer to have.

They were the best team in the country, Everton were champions, but Liverpool were THE club. They actually came in for me in the January, but I had always said that I wanted to stay at Watford until the end of the season. With that, it looked to many as if I had snubbed Liverpool and that wasn't the done thing.

So, when I did sign, and when I started training and playing pre-season games, I got a bit of stick from some fans who thought I had messed their club about. Liverpool wanted me earlier because they were challenging for the title with Everton, but I had agreed to stay at Watford and then I listened to the talk about Arsenal. All in all it looked as though I wasn't completely happy with my move to Anfield, but of course I was. Back then, if Liverpool came in for you, no one else might as well have bothered. That's that, you're going to Liverpool.

I sensed that slight animosity, but the best thing that could have happened was that our first three league games were away from home because there was a hole on the Kop. That was perfect because by the time I got to Anfield I had set up a goal at Arsenal, scored at Coventry and played well. The fans had taken to me on our travels and any bad feeling had gone.

A lot too was made of the colour of my skin. Howard Gayle had made a handful of appearances in the early 1980s, but I was the first established black player to arrive at Anfield. It wasn't an issue for me. Let me tell you, I grew up playing at Millwall and West Ham and if a young black player could play there in the early 1980s, he could play anywhere. The way I saw it was, the only way my colour would have been an issue is if I hadn't performed well. If I was poor, it would have been because of my colour. If you're white and you don't do well, it's just because you're crap. If you're black, it's because you're black! That's how some people think. It's sad, but it's true.

A guy who later became a good pal of mine in Liverpool used to go to Anfield every week. He sat near these two old Scousers; they must have been about 60 and had been going to Anfield for 50-odd years. From the January, when it became apparent that the club wanted me, they were always saying, "We don't want him here, we don't want him at this club." This went on and on. "We shouldn't have black players at this club, it's not right." Anyway, the season starts, I've done well away from home and then on my first game at Anfield, I've played great and I score a free kick, bang, into the top corner. Amid all the cheering and chanting of my name, one of the guys turns to the other and says, "Hey lad, he's not as black as I thought."

IT WAS A new adventure for me, but also a new adventure for Liverpool and a new chapter in their history. Kenny Dalglish had come in, won the double in his first season in charge, but soon realised that he needed to make changes to an ageing side. He had all but retired, Rushie had gone and other teams were catching up. It needed tinkering with. I arrived, John Aldridge and Nigel Spackman had been there a few months and then Peter Beardsley was brought in for a lot of money. Ray Houghton would arrive later for £800,000. It was a totally new approach. The club had always had continuity; they bought young players and let them make their way in slowly. They had a mainstay of established players, and then they brought in individuals who would complement what they already had.

Now suddenly, we were established players arriving. Beardsley was a record signing at £1.9m, Aldo had scored loads and was replacing Rush, and I was an England international. This put a lot of pressure on our shoulders, but from the first day in pre-season you could tell this was going to be good, we all clicked and I couldn't wait to get started.

We lost 3-2 away at Bayern Munich in our first pre-season friendly, but we played great and Bayern had already started their season. From there we gelled on and off the pitch. OK so footballers always gel off the pitch, let's be fair; but this was special.

I don't know what I expected when I arrived. Maybe I thought there would be some sort of initiation into *the* Liverpool way. You arrive thinking, "What's the secret?" and then what happens is you're thrown a bib and told, "That's your team." It was five-a-sides all day, that's all we did. It fascinated and amazed me because you think there'll be this big myth, but the only secret was signing good players who could play together. That was the "secret", it was that simple. It had been blatantly obvious to everyone for years!

That was training; five-a-sides, a few sprints and more five-a-sides. Bruce Grobbelaar would play outfield, he never did any goalkeeping practice. The games were with small goals and no keepers, so Bruce was on the wing. He was good actually. He would be great now that keepers aren't allowed to pick the ball up.

I had come from Watford under Graham Taylor, a well-organised and tactical set up. We had our jobs to do and a specific method of play. At Liverpool it was just, "Go out and play". I thought I would have to learn how to play in that cohesive way of theirs, but no, it was a case of gelling. They gave tips but no coaching.

As I say, the team had done well in their first three games away from Anfield and I felt good about the way I had been playing. It was vital for me to start well, and I think that goes for all players. If you start well, they'll forgive you down the line; if you start badly at a club, you're in trouble. An example is Harry Kewell. He's a good player, but he hasn't started well. He's been upset by injuries and that's affected his performances when he has made it on to the pitch. So now, if he goes on and has three great games, but his fourth is poor, they'll be those fans saying, "I told you he was crap." And he'll probably be crap because he's an Aussie.

FORTUNATELY FOR ME, though, things went so well from the off. I felt so at home in the team, at the club, in the city and among the players I was with. We played QPR in October and that was another fantastic day. They were top of the table, a good side, but we took them to pieces and I managed two cracking goals. I always liked scoring against David Seaman as he was such a quality keeper.

That day highlighted how well we'd clicked as a team and just how fluid we could be. I don't want to sound like a broken record, but again, it was down to the five-a-sides. It's all about passing and moving and it's all about attacking from different angles. Steve Nicol got loads of goals and couldn't stop scoring early on and that was from defensive positions. The way we trained transferred itself out on to the pitch.

Our centre-backs, Alan Hansen, Mark Lawrenson and Gary Ablett were so comfortable both in defence and on the ball that everyone else could get on with the business of attacking. Ronnie Whelan could sit in if he liked, but everyone from Steve Nicol to McMahon, to Ray Houghton, we all concentrated on getting forward and that was just so exciting.

It was a great midfield and again slightly different from the usual Liverpool way of doing things. They had been used to having four hard working midfielders across the middle. Sammy Lee, Souness, Whelan, Case, Ray Kennedy even. But when I came I was different, I was an attacker playing in midfield.

People compare teams and I always said that the Liverpool sides of the 1970s and early 1980s were much stronger, but we had more flair. They had been labelled as a machine that ground teams down and won trophy after trophy. Our team were still winning, but playing attractive football that hadn't been seen before.

It was such a pleasure and so effective. We could annihilate teams on our day. I was allowed to drift. Kenny never told me how to play. I could drift into inside-left knowing that Steve Nicol, who started the season at left-back behind me, would make runs past me. I didn't have to be an out and out winger. Steve Nicol could play all over the place, but I liked playing with him more than any other full back.

WITH EVERYTHING GOING so well and game after game being won and won in style, the "pundits" had crowned us champions by Christmas. The club had a different approach though and eventual success was very low key. I soon realised that there is no ceremony about titles. "Here's your medal, pre-season is on the 12th July." Apparently it had been the same since Shankly. That was that, so you never took anything for granted. Ambition was never talked about and certainly never achieved. There was *always* next year and that was their big thing. Again, again, again.

We lost to Arsenal the following season 2-0 in the last minute to blow the league title in the last game on our own pitch at Anfield. It was a crazy night. There were a couple of rows, some disappointment, but then it was over, and it was on to next year. We won it back. Manchester United had that in the 1990s I think.

Success and defeat were treated in very similar ways. We were content with how well it was going, but we knew we had games to play. Not until we played the game that won the title in 1988 did I even think about myself as a champion. It wasn't a conscious thing, I just loved playing for that team, and so it mattered little if some people thought it was all over. What I loved was crossing over the white line and playing with those guys. It could have been a pre-season friendly, it didn't matter to me. It was a joy. Coming into training, you knew you were going to have a good time. It was a schoolboy's dream. We were like a bunch of kids, playing laughing and seemingly every Saturday, winning.

WITH THOSE VICTORIES some people's attentions were fixated on a record set by Leeds United in 1974 of 29 games unbeaten in a season. We didn't think about it at all until I was told it would be Everton that we would have to visit and come away with a result from to break the record. Then you start wondering. But to me it was a nothing record. OK, if you go through the whole season unbeaten like Arsenal in 2004/05, that is special, but 29 games, so what? It sounded good, but it was just another boring stat. We lost at Everton and only equalled Leeds' record, but it was disappointing to me because we lost to Everton, nothing else. We had lost a derby match. That hurt. All season sounds good, 29, who cares?

In fact losing that game set up a trio of games in 11 days against Nottingham Forest that would shape the season. They were a very good team and had a great manager in Brian Clough. They played attractive football and they were pressing for honours. There was a big rivalry between the two clubs that had been a left over from the 1970s when both were vying for the European Cup.

Now that rivalry was between two teams playing the best football in the country. George Graham's Arsenal had arrived on the scene, but they played in a different way to Forest and ourselves.

The first of the matches was at the City Ground in the First Division. Forest played well and beat us 2-1. Steve Chettle was their young right-back. I didn't play well there and there were big headlines in the papers, "I'LL HAVE BARNES ON TOAST". Chettle had supposedly said to a paper how he was going to put the shackles on me again in the semi-final on the following Saturday. He probably never said it, but that's how it works. It fired me up though, I can tell you. There was a lot of focus on me, and I had a bit of niggle about the whole thing. It gave me an extra bit of fizz for that semi.

Steve was a bit sheepish in the cup game and perhaps a bit embarrassed. I had a good game, we won 2-1 and I had a hand in both our goals. I remember Clough wasn't best pleased with poor Chettle for that newspaper article and I actually felt a little sorry for him.

THE GAME AT Anfield then was all set up. Each team had won one and each game had been a good closely-fought football match. It was a more relaxed build up for me after settling that score with Chettle, but there was still a bit of niggle between the two sides and anyway, if we won that night the title was effectively ours.

Kenny's new Liverpool team was a great unit and, as good as Forest were, not many teams could live with us. In goal, Brucie was excellent. I don't know how but he was a natural. He was a good height, not too big. He was a good athlete, he could play basketball, he could juggle, he had great hands, some will recall he could even walk on them.

The back four was both strong and accomplished on the ball. As I said, I liked playing with Steve Nicol at left-back behind me. What was happening down the right though was that Barry Venison and Ray Houghton were very steady. Ray could tuck in and Barry was defensive. Kenny thought that if he put Steve Nicol down the right he could replicate that attacking drive and give the team some balance. Steve was never as attacking down the right though, which was strange as he was right-footed.

In the heart of the midfield was Steve McMahon. He was such a Scouser, a real niggler. He wasn't the most popular player with the Forest boys, Stuart Pearce particularly. There had been a few barneys between the two on England duty. In a later game, Brian Laws got into a scuffle with Aldo near the Forest box. We all got involved and Pearcey has run across the pitch, we all part like the sea for him and he's grabbed Laws saying; "Never mind about fucking John Aldridge, get McMahon!"

Macca thrived off of it though. There are some players who you need to put your arm around and cajole, not Macca. You had to wind him up and get him excited to get the best out of him and that wasn't too difficult.

Ronnie Whelan had been injured so Macca had Nigel Spackman alongside him. I rated Nigel. He was more mobile than Ronnie and his tidy style suited the team. Like Ronnie, his role in the middle with Macca was vital because they both won us so much possession.

We had a great balance, but then again so did Forest. Clough junior was dangerous. Forest deployed him just off the front man and it was a fairly new thing. That made Nigel very dangerous. Who picks him up? He used to find a lot of space. His problem by dropping there was that he came up against Steve McMahon.

Stuart Pearce had broken into the England set-up and was a fiercely competitive left-back. I think he struggled against us a little though because in Ray Houghton he didn't have an out-and-out winger to chase, tackle and, if needs be, kick. I think he would have preferred to have been marking me to be honest.

Ray played on Pearce's insecurity and would come inside, and that flummoxed Pearcey because he never knew where Houghton would pop up. Pearcey would have done better against me as my role was more defined and I didn't defend as well as Ray.

Neil Webb was a quality England international midfielder and the in the centre of their defence Forest had England centre-half Des Walker. He hated playing against Peter Beardsley though. Des's whole thing was his ability to defend deep and clean up behind his defensive partner. People would launch balls to a centre-forward and whether the attacker won it or not, Des's pace would make sure the danger was mopped up.

Against us he had to think again about his natural game. Des would say about Peter, "I hate playing against that little bastard," because Peter wasn't attacking constantly, Peter was all over the place and that took Des's ability out of the equation. Because of that I felt that Peter was our most instrumental player when it came to playing Forest. In the semi-final that year, we scored a lovely goal where I crossed it for Aldo, but it was Peter who had dropped deep and put me in.

WITH PLENTY OF great players on show the atmosphere at Anfield was good. The crowd were up for it. We were Wembley bound, and they were relishing another cracking game. Regardless of position or form, we always had good matches against Forest. It would always be tidy. Forest were never spoilers, they wouldn't come and try and stop us playing, they wanted to get on with their own game and our fans appreciated that.

In fact it was their intention, I think, to really get at us. The cup defeat still smarted with them big time and their young players had a point to prove. We knew that from the off it was going to be a high tempo match. Pearcey was kicking and fighting for the ball, but we knew we could let them tire themselves out and so we got on with our simple passing game and managed to get into our stride. Everything just clicked - it was ridiculous. Even Aldo was flicking the ball about and let me tell you, in five-a-sides, you wouldn't have Aldo in your team. He was a great goalscorer, one of the best, but not much use on the ball; or so I thought. That night he looked like Platini.

WE HAD A couple of half-chances in the early exchanges, but took the lead in the 18th minute. Hansen strode out of defence like only he could and played in Ray. He played a one-two with me before slipping the ball under Steve Sutton in the Forest goal. It was a typical Liverpool goal.

We all liked to go toward the ball and receive it. Aldo was the only one who wanted it through or over the top. It's like Arsenal today; we never put the ball aimlessly into the box. That's how we played. Ray and myself could come inside and so there would be four or five players in a small area. That's where our one touch stuff came into its own, as there's so little space in that final third and we could kill teams around the box.

Unlike me, Ray wasn't a dribbler, but he was great at one-twos and could get in behind a defence with a quick couple of passes. Forest were coming in to tackle so quickly and the one touch stuff had to be crisp, and it was that night. It all came off. We were a good side, but we weren't good enough to do that every week, not at that high level. That night, though, everything came off.

Ray had been an important addition to the squad and the team. Craig Johnston was such an energetic player, but Kenny saw something in Ray that he felt would aid the team that bit more. Kenny's amazing, though. He sees things in players that others don't. He signed Jon Dahl Thomson who, OK, didn't score goals at Newcastle, but he went on to score plenty in World Cups and at AC Milan. He's a great player and Kenny had seen that.

Ray wasn't skilful, quick or tall, but he was so intelligent and so good on the ball as a passer. He would make such great runs. Think Freddie Ljungberg today. Ray would come from wide and run across the pitch before darting in. He wasn't a get to the byline man like me, he would drift and that upsets defenders.

AS FOR HANSEN, who created the first goal, what a player. I personally feel the demise of Liverpool was down to Alan retiring. He started so many of our attacks by gliding out of defence, but that was because he couldn't kick the ball more than 30 yards. He was so comfortable and as he came out we would all show for him. That was Alan's problem with Scotland. He would come out with the ball looking for a player, but they often didn't show. He would lose it and they would lose a goal. At Liverpool we all knew him and his style was the start of so much of our play. I think Ron Atkinson had a good record against Liverpool because he would always harass his forwards to press Hansen and stop him getting things started from the back. Alan has never been properly replaced, but then there aren't many defenders with his quality on the ball. In fact I can only think of one really and that's Franz Beckenbauer.

We continued to play the ball about at pace and there was nothing the Forest boys could do, and they were working hard I can tell you. In the 38th minute, Peter dropped deep, Des is nowhere and Aldo, higher up the pitch, is one-on-one with Colin Foster. Peter's pass was sublime and opened up the defence and there was Aldo in on goal, nonchalantly lifting the ball over Sutton and into the net. I told you, Platini.

Aldo was not particularly quick, but he always got on the end of a pass. How? Rushie's pace was obvious, but with Aldo, his timing was so spot on that he had a head start. I knew Aldo was good, but when he went to Spain I felt he might struggle a bit as it is so technical there, but he scored a lot of goals out there and that underlined how good a player and what an intelligent and gifted forward he was.

We may have been 2-0 up just before half-time, but we were enjoying it that much that there was no let up. Even our hardman Steve McMahon got in on the act and with one incredible swivel of the hips he sold the Forest boys a dazzling dummy but this time unfortunately Aldo couldn't quite live up to the build-up and the chance had gone.

THERE WERE MORE though. Peter was majorly in the mood and one scintillating dribble took him past four defenders with that characteristic shoulder drop of his and he smashed the ball on to the bar bringing the Anfield crowd to their feet. Those fans have seen plenty of quality over the years and it takes something to get them up, but that night Peter had them out of their seats.

The team's flair and Peter's form had even me switching wings and just before half-time I found myself on the right flank where I managed to step over the ball and slip Beardsley in on goal. Peter's drive was saved by Sutton, but having strayed I could only watch from the turf as Pearcey came through me with a right whack. "I'm staying on the left", I decided and that was the last time I got near Mr Pearce.

Sutton's save underlined what a good keeper he was and how well he was playing. You got used to that Anfield. Often keepers would have incredible matches at our place because they were so in demand. You often find that keepers of relegated teams are named their club's "Player of the Season" and that's because they have so much to do. Forest, of course, were nowhere near the relegation battles back then (they finished third that season), but Sutton was great and if it wasn't for him it would have been seven or eight that night.

The tempo of the game was so impressive and, strangely, a lot of that was due to Forest's tactics and determination. We were fortunate in that, as much as Forest tried, their game plan was not working; it was playing into our hands. Because of that we could keep the ball from them and make them suffer. They didn't have a ball-winner in the middle. Usually they could get away with it because their opponents would lose it and hand them possession back; not us, not that night. We kept the ball for such long periods and there was not much they could do about it.

We went in at half-time a happy team, but there was no admiration, no patting each other on the back. We were two up in a First Division match and that was that. Sure, we'd played phenomenally well, but that wasn't going to last another 45 minutes. It couldn't, could it? There was never much praise from the staff, just pragmatic orders to keep focused and to keep doing what we had been doing.

WE WENT OUT to attack the Kop. I never really thought much about the advantages of attacking our famous end. It certainly never made me more geed up. It was great, don't get me wrong, but I loved both ends and did very well going at the Anfield Road stand. I suppose, though, it was always nice to score in front of the Kop and after ten minutes we did exactly that from an unlikely source.

Gary Gillespie must have been up for a corner and was on hand to drill the ball high into the net after more great stuff along the by-line from Peter. Gary had suffered with injury, but he was a very good player. He was 6ft 4in tall, but wasn't into the physical side of things. He wanted the ball at his feet and, like Alan, was very comfortable on it. They defended by stealth rather than by presence. They would glide attackers away from the danger areas.

That's maybe why we struggled with Wimbledon in that's season's FA Cup final, because their forwards were well up for a fight. I remember Gillespie's goal against Forest well because of Gary's crap celebration. He knelt down and pointed to the sky. Typical defender, no idea about a cool celebration.

At 3-0 we were immediately settled. Des Walker went off injured, but at 2-0 there is that worry that despite all our good work they could get one and we're back in a battle. Gary's goal calmed all those fears and we could relax and get on playing our stuff. Forest were now totally deflated.

We wouldn't take the piss, not consciously. We would never try and take the piss. It might have looked like we were, but we never disrespected the opposition. We just got ourselves into positions that allowed us to do things that made us look good and sometimes inevitably the opposition look bad.

That's what happened with our fourth goal. Nigel Spackman played the ball quite wide to the left and I was by the corner flag with Chettle facing me. That was the first time I had ever deliberately meant to nutmeg a player. I never usually went for one because I liked to dribble and I always thought that if a nutmeg fails then I've lost the ball. "What if he doesn't open his legs?"

Jan Molby was the master at it, but not me. This time, though, Chettle launched himself at me. He should have jockeyed me as I was in a tight spot, but for some reason he came in to kick me. Maybe he was still wanting me on toast. I didn't want to nutmeg him, I wanted to dribble round him, but he forced my hand, I swear.

I'm on the ball, he's coming at me and he's coming with pace. "He's going to kick me," I thought, and, as he launched in, the natural thing to do was slip it through his legs. Then, as I went by him, Gary Crosby came sliding in. I liked it when the midfield player was an attacking type because they are easier to go past. Dennis Wise would double up on me and that was hard as he was a good defensive player. Gary Crosby though threw himself in and I could just get by. I nudged it past him and then from the byline I pulled it back and Peter faded a great shot into the net.

Peter's finish was fantastic and it was a goal he so deserved. He was my favourite player to play with. I loved Peter. We got some stick for saying we only ever passed to each other. I don't know if that was true but we always played on the same team in training, he would always look for me. Peter was so selfless though. We roomed together for England and Liverpool and had a special bond. As for my role in that goal, it was a nice moment. It was good to get along the byline and look to get someone in for a shot. Sir Tom Finney was there that night and I'm sure he liked that sort of wing play and he said some nice things afterwards about the team and me.

I ALWAYS GOT more pleasure from setting up goals than I did scoring them. That was why I could never be an out-and-out goalscorer. I played up there for Watford, Liverpool, and England. I was the First Division's top scorer in 1990 with 29 goals, but I preferred to set them up. I look at Thierry Henry today and, yeah, he's a great goalscorer, but I get the feeling he loves to create chances, he loves to pull wide, beat players and create. Michael Owen and Ruud van Nistelrooy, they're different, they want to score goals and that's it, but I liked to do both and that assured me that I was not an out and out centre-forward like some people thought I might be. I'd rather have lots of touches of the ball, be involved in all the play and beat some people than do nothing all match and score a couple. That's why I enjoyed this match so much because I was so involved and, although I didn't find the net myself, I was creating, interacting and a big part of the team.

We continued to dominate. When everyone is doing so well, and everything is coming off, confidence is such a big factor and you try things you usually wouldn't and invariably they come off. With only a few of minutes left, Nigel Spackman, not someone you usually see in the opposition box, took the ball from Peter and again pulled it across the goal for Aldo to score his second and our fifth.

After that we kept the ball for such long spells of possession. I've played and been on the end of hammerings when the opposition have the ball for five-minute spells and the crowd are cheering "Ole". It's not nice, but we were having ten-minute spells with the ball and I'm sure that was tough on Forest.

The closest I felt to that was in an FA Cup semi-final for Watford in 1987 when Spurs took an early 3-0 lead. That was hard and I remember Glenn Hoddle coming over to me, patting me on the backside and saying, "Keep going, Digger." He wasn't taking the piss he was just being nice, but I thought, "How low can you get? Even the opposition are feeling sorry for me." That was how I imagine the Forest boys felt because they were getting a run-around.

I didn't want the game to end. It was one of those matches. It could have been tiring because we had so much of the ball, but it would have been a pleasure to have played all night. I loved football then. It wasn't an individual thing, I just loved the team. I loved the way we played, I loved the way our team flowed and moved.

Afterwards we knew that game had been something special. "Come in for some light training tomorrow," said Ronnie Moran. That was that. No histrionics, no praise. "Well done and let's move forward."

I HAVE OFTEN wondered how the Forest dressing room was after that game, but I never talked to Pearcey or the other guys about it. Clough, though, was no fool, was he? He knew that his good, young side had just met a fine team, who that night got everything right.

I suppose it was a shame that we couldn't compete in Europe because of the ban still in force after the Heysel disaster, but that was the situation and there was no point losing sleep over it. We could have come up against the great AC Milan team that housed the brilliant Dutch trio of Marco van Basten, Frank Rijkaard, and Rudd Gullit. I'm not one for meaningless comparisons, but that would have been a great match.

I think they were more powerful than us, although I think we might have been a bit more fluid. They had great players, but were also very strong and very direct if needs be. They had hard working men as well, Ancelotti and Donadoni. It would have been their power against our guile and whether or not our defenders would have been able to handle Gullit and van Basten.

Who knows? But what I am sure of is that the Forest game was the most pleasing game I ever played in and it came in my most memorable season. It was my first year at Liverpool, I was apprehensive but it all just fell into place. To win the title was incredible and although you never get complacent about winning honours, your first is always nice.

As for that game, I could sit and watch it again and again. The whole 90 minutes are so watchable and whenever I stick the video on I am drawn in. Arsène Wenger's Arsenal recently reached the sort of level that we played that night, but I'm not sure they have ever achieved it for the whole match.

It was a special night and a special team. I won't ever forget either.

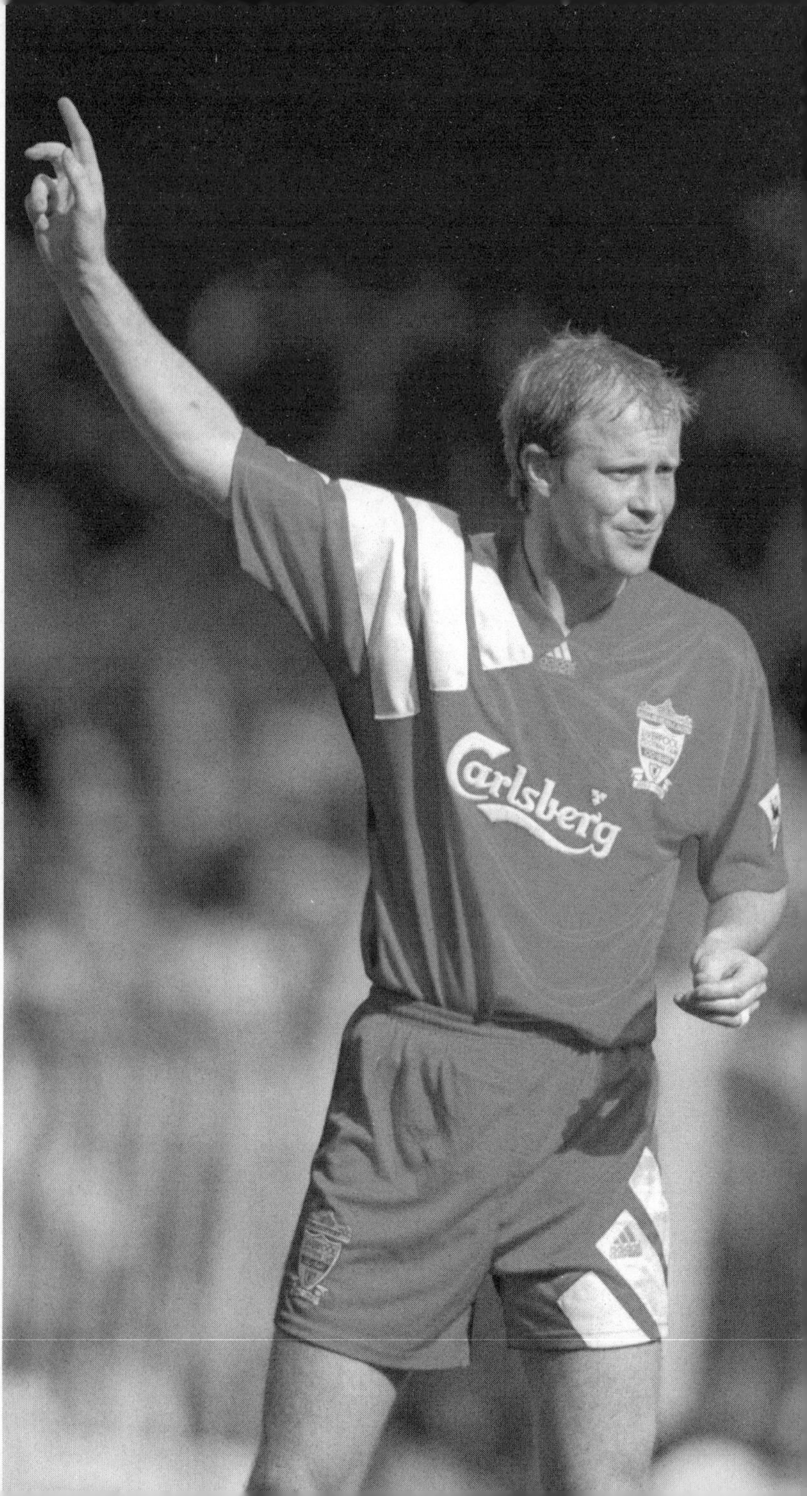

MARK WRIGHT: BORN 1 AUGUST 1963, BERINSFIELD; 210 GAMES, 7 GOALS

Mark Wright

Liverpool 2 Paris St Germain 0
Cup Winners' Cup semi-final second leg
Wednesday 24 April 1997

THE GAME I recall with the fondest of memories from my time at
Liverpool Football Club is a strange one, because ultimately it ended
in failure and that isn't a word you often associate with the place.

The second leg of the 1997 European Cup Winners' Cup semi-
final at Anfield, though, was a special occasion, and one I will never
forget. We had been beaten by three goals to nil in Paris and, as we
set about righting that wrong, I experienced the sort of night Anfield
is famous for. Sure, we didn't quite get there, but the passion, the
excitement, the fervour of the team, it was never bettered during
the six wonderful years I spent at the club and, because of that, it
is this match - labelled "the impossible dream" by the local paper -
that evokes my greatest memory of my time at Anfield.

People may raise an eyebrow to that. After all I captained the
team to the FA Cup in 1992, but that victory against Second
Division Sunderland was so expected, so one-sided even, that it
lacked the excitement that a football match can bring us players.
Wembley was great, don't get me wrong, and I was as proud as any
captain before or since to lift that famous trophy in a Liverpool
shirt, but European nights at Anfield with those fans cheering us
on, that was special. That meant something and in many ways was
the reason I joined this great old club.

I ARRIVED IN the summer of 1991, but could have been a
Liverpool player much sooner. Kenny Dalglish had wanted to bring
me to the club and whilst I was very flattered, I had a lot of time

for Arthur Cox, the manager at my then club Derby and the good people of that town. Looking back now, of course, I think "How silly, I should have signed then! I might have won the league." I won 45 England caps, but I should have got 80; you can have regret after regret, but things happen for a reason.

I signed once Graeme Souness had taken over as manager and, what with the changes happening at the club, I suppose it was inevitable that comparisons were made between the new players coming in and those who had left. I was talked about in relation to Alan Hansen, which made me laugh. If you get talked about in the same category as Alan Hansen, you feel you must be doing something right. Alan was the benchmark for centre-halves as far as I was concerned. He was quality but he also won loads. I didn't. I can't be talked about in the same breath as Alan. It's nice if people make comparisons, but to me they are futile. I always saw myself as more of a ball winner than Alan anyway. He was far silkier than me; silkier than anybody.

Maybe then, because of those comparisons and because I shared that role as the man at the back, Graeme immediately made me team captain. I had been skipper everywhere I'd played and so I think Graeme saw something in me. Looking back, maybe it was too soon. Liverpool is a unique set-up. I really wanted it, but there is a back room thing at the club and there is a way of doing things. I was aware that you should step up through the ranks, but here I was immediately being made captain.

That was Graeme, though. He wanted to do so well and he changed so much, so quickly. He was eager and some of the lads didn't like it. Legends like Whelan, Rush, Molby, Nicol; they had been at the club for ages and, with hindsight, me being made captain upset a few of them; it caused problems with those old-school players. The new boys were fine, but it concerned some that here I was, the new boy, not going through the usual procedure.

I wanted to be captain and I had nothing but pride when I led that team out, but it might have been better for Graeme to keep the guys together. He should have kept the chain of command, but he broke it and with that came problems.

The old lads would make it slightly difficult for the new guys, but there was nothing novel in that. That had always been the way and it was part of the system of initiation, if you like. You had to earn the right to be part of the team and I had no problem with that. Here I was, I'd cost a lot of money, over £2m, but I had won nothing and so I had to prove myself. That's football and that's right. They had been bought up at the club and of course they were going to be annoyed. Why should they bow down to a new guy? There will always be cliques at a football club, that's the way it is, but I think me being made skipper caused a rift and it became the old school versus the new players. It became a case of us and them. Kids must clean boots and learn to respect the team and I think the same should go for new players.

The thing is though, I've arrived from Derby County, I'm asked if I would captain Liverpool Football Club, what am I going to say? "Thanks, but I think there is a way of doing things and this ain't it?" No. I said, "Yes, please, Graeme" because it is such an honour and all the shit that comes with it will just have to sort itself out. If I'd thought too much about it, I might have worried, but I was so proud that I said "of course" straight away.

We won the FA Cup that year and that papered over the cracks, but then we had to come back for a new season and start again and those cracks hadn't gone away. The thing was, Graeme was a winner, but I think he lacked a bit of patience. He was so eager and changed so much that it became difficult to keep a unity within the team. In hindsight, I think he wouldn't't have changed so much and particularly so many of the personnel. Maybe he would have been subtler and let it evolve in time instead of coming in and doing so much so quickly. He did that, though, because he cared so much. It just turned out to be the wrong move.

Graeme was strong enough to know what he wants and do it. He knew that he would upset some legends, but he knew a lot of them were coming to the end of their days there and changes had to be made. He had inherited an old team from Kenny Dalglish and it took a strong man to go through with the changes which were obviously necessary, but quite unpopular all the same. Unfortunately, results didn't match those brave decisions. It led to Graeme's well-documented heart problems, triple bypass surgery and within three years of arriving at Anfield Graeme left the club without seeing any of his changes come to fruition.

ROY EVANS WAS a hugely popular figure of the back room team and knew the club inside and out. The club looked to go back to the boot room, the basics that the club had thought they had lost with Souness. The thing is, and I can't speak for other players I can only speak for me, Roy was too nice a man. I'm in management now; can I be the players' mate? No, I can't. Can I go round to their houses for Sunday dinner? No I can't. He got too close to some of the lads and when you do that, where is your edge?

You have to be strong in today's game, but you could understand that Roy was seen as the best man for the job because the club wanted that old unity that had stood them in such good stead for so long.

He was so enthusiastic and so energetic, though. The club was about buying the best and so didn't need any clever coaching. You had to be a man-manager with the side and, whilst Roy was great with the lads, it just didn't work out for him because of the reasons I have highlighted. That's my opinion.

Roy inherited a very good squad of players. Graeme's legacy must be the chance he gave to so many good young players. That again was a change. How often did you see teenagers playing for Liverpool when they were dominating? Now we had Steve McManaman, Robbie Fowler, Rob Jones, and Jamie Redknapp, all thrown together in the team and they were doing very well. Under Roy, those same players blossomed and he built a team around them and their talents.

Should those talents have achieved more? Was that team guilty of underachieving? Maybe so, that's up to history to decide, but I think that we should have won more. I think you can look back on that team and say that yeah, we underachieved. We were close to winning the Premiership and things went against us, but we also lacked certain things that you need to be champions.

We could have done with another keeper to keep David James on his toes. That was key. There were certain games that we lost when we should have won, and in 1996/97, when we eventually came fourth, I really think we were the best side, but we lacked a cutting edge and eventually threw away points willy-nilly and ended up with nothing.

I FEEL SAD that we didn't't do more for Liverpool Football Club and the brilliant fans, but you can't harbour regrets for life. Football is a bloody hard game. We thought that we were good enough, but the records say that we weren't't and they're what count.

I felt sorry for Roy. The players have to take some of the blame and, whilst trying to win this club honours, the manager also had to deal with the "Spice Boy" label given to his team.

The lads took some stick and I think a lot of it, whilst over the top, was very fair. They were all out and about, they were all into their designer gear, some were flying off to do catwalk shows on the continent, and to me that's not football.

I don't doubt their desire for the game, but it was frustrating to see them get so wrapped up in all the paraphernalia surrounding the club back then. Young footballers were all the rage. Lad mags celebrated their every move, there were girls and parties and clothes and drinks and I was probably just jealous that an old-timer like myself was never invited to these lavish bashes! I was never going to be on the catwalk, was I?

They got carried away though. I don't think the boys went out and consciously set about it knowing that it would affect their football, but it did. Course it did.

The older players suggested to them to calm down a bit, but when you're young and going out to meet the pop-stars and the models, who's going to listen? You're getting flown out to Milan with all the five star treatment and Mark Wright has a quiet word in your ear to maybe concentrate on your football. Are you going to listen? Course you're bloody not.

I suppose the biggest example of being side-tracked was the white suit debacle at Wembley before the FA Cup final in 1996. That was David James. He had a contact at Armani. I was expecting them in grey and suddenly they turn up and they're white. I'm no fashion expert, but a white suit ain't going to suit me that's for sure.

I'm like, "What the hell is that?" Can you imagine the likes of Alan Hansen, Tommy Smith, Graeme Souness, or Jimmy Case putting white suits on? That ilk of a man wouldn't be seen dead in one and here I am having to wear the bloody thing.

Neil Ruddock, Jones, Phil Babb, they loved it and all had the designer sunnies on, but I knew we had lost our edge that afternoon. Manchester United would have looked at us and thought "posers" and given that little bit more. We played shit and lost.

For all of that, I thought we had a great team. Real talent flowed through that side and that's what makes it even more frustrating. Despite all that we played some fantastic stuff, that's for sure. I have many fond memories about the way we played and some of the individual performances in that side. Robbie was a dream to play with, Jamie was a great young pro, Macca was a real talent, but I was at Liverpool to win and I just felt that we lacked a cutting edge; "The Eye of the Tiger". That little bit of hunger that you need to succeed was missing and that cost us dear.

WE STARTED THE 1996/97 wanting to improve on the season before and were confident that we could bring the club the honours it yearned for after so many barren years. Looking back there was such a desire to do well and that may have deterred us from our objective. I think Manchester United suffered with that desperation to win the title for so long before they did and at Liverpool then the talk was always of how well we must do this time.

In the past it had been seamless. Liverpool could see a weakness three years before it became one. They would highlight it, go out and buy someone, stick them in the reserves and by the time that problem arose they had a player there ready to step in. Incredible.

Roy was a throwback to those glory days, as was Ronnie Moran. Ronnie was always after me, always on my case telling me what I should be doing, I might have felt that I was an international and didn't need advice, but now I am a manager I know exactly what he was trying to do. If someone else did something wrong, it was me he shouted at. He could talk to other people, but talk about you and know you were listening. It was his way of having a go, keeping you on your toes.

The young players learnt a lot from the previous campaign when we played some great stuff and on our day looked the best team in the country. We won home and away against United, who won the double, and won with style against Arsenal, Villa and, memorably, Newcastle.

A big part of that success was Robbie Fowler. What a player! Robbie was the most natural goalscorer that I have played with, ever. Ian Rush, Gary Lineker, they were great, but Robbie, he was the best. If you could see him in training it was unbelievable. Watch him in shooting practice was something to behold. Either foot and the accuracy? It was an incredible sight. He went off the rails a bit, but he was a Liverpool lad and there was a lot on his plate. I have nothing but admiration for Robbie. I always will.

Stan Collymore too was a fine player, but I look back at his spell at Liverpool and it just annoys me. Stan was more than frustrating. I still think the boy's a fool. I think he's an idiot. He was a fool to himself. Look at the facts. He was 6ft 2 in. He had a right foot and a left foot. He could head the ball, he had pace, he was strong, he could be nasty when he needed to be and do you know what he achieved? Nothing. Anybody with that amount of god-given talent and who achieves nothing is a fool. He is a wasted talent and that is an awful example to everybody out there.

When he first arrived at the club and I watched him train, I thought "Wow, what a player, this kid has everything." But then, whoosh, he throws it away. He got too much money and wasted himself. I don't know what happened, but my opinion is that he didn't want it enough. If you want it, you don't get side-tracked, but he allowed himself to let it slip. It's just silly and I ain't got time for people who waste their talents. Talents that most would die for.

LIKE STAN, THAT team let their promise lie dormant, but whilst we dropped away in that season's title race after it had looked like ours for the taking, we excelled in Europe and, after three fairly easy victories in the opening rounds, found ourselves in the semi-final of the European Cup Winners' Cup against Paris St Germain.

The first leg, though, was a disaster. Roy got it wrong. I hate to say it, but we were naïve that night. I didn't't agree with some of the things that had been said beforehand, but what do you do? You are a player and you get on with it. In my opinion you have to shut up shop out there. All campaign in Europe we had played one up front away from home, but in Paris both Stan and Robbie played.

We hadn't watched any of their games, the preparation wasn't there and we arrived with the attitude that we could get after them. That's all very well and brave, but it is naïve. They weren't't going to be in the semi-final of the Cup Winners' Cup unless they were a good side and I think PSG were underestimated and that was unusual. Chasing the game left us open to the counter-attack and they picked us off.

We got beat 3-0 and I think it could have been more. It was a very difficult night. They got on top from the beginning and we found it hard. John Barnes and myself were talking, trying to change the way we approached the game, but it was too late and the damage was done. I was so disappointed. We knew it wasn't right. It was a brave decision to get at them, but I knew and others knew that it was the wrong one.

WE WOULD HAVE to make changes if we were to have any chance of turning this around. The players changed the tactics. That was the good thing about Roy. Sure, at the end of the day it was his decision, but we got amongst him and he listened to our suggestions. That was nice.

Ronnie Moran was also very instrumental. "What do you think, guys?" he asked. We all sat around and the players said that we have no choice now to go after them, pressure them high up the pitch and not let them play football. The full-backs were told to bomb on, leave me and Razor at the back. If the two of us couldn't handle that, then none of us should be playing for Liverpool.

We went two-for-two at the back and we held such a high line. All they could do was launch it long and Razor and I could just head it back in to the mix and we could start to pressure them again.

Barnesy was dropped. He loved to play football, he was in the centre of midfield by then and he always wanted the ball at his feet and he always wanted to get things going; to feet, to feet, to feet. He was such a fine player, but that wasn't the night to be pretty, we had to get after them and pin them in.

With Michael Thomas holding the middle with Jamie, we had four attacking options in Patrick Berger, Macca, Robbie and Collymore. We absolutely battered them. At times it was route one. When we had the ball we would get in, they'd clear it, we'd have the ball again and we'd hump it in. That's how it went. Like the Alamo.

In training they told you about nights past and how the Kop could suck the ball into the net, but they also wanted us focused on the matter at hand and that's what we were. What we all were aware of, though, was the role that the fans could play in getting us up for the job at hand and, my word, did they live up to expectations.

IT WAS NEVER seen as a lost cause, there wasn't such a thing at Anfield, not among those fans. We walked out of the tunnel and their passion hit you smack between the eyes. These people truly believed that we could do it, turn round this three-goal deficit and that rubbed off on us. I suppose it was the same for the boys in Istanbul. Those fans have a funny effect on us footballers and if they believe, so will I. There were scarves, flags, singing; it's funny, why can't there be atmosphere like that every Saturday?

I don't know what the French thought of it all. Perhaps they had heard what effect it had had on their countrymen St Etienne in 1977. We felt we knew enough to ruffle them. They weren't used to playing against high backlines, and facing attacking full-backs. Why play a continental way? It has always baffled me, why play these teams and try and match them for style? The English game is about high pressure, fitness and getting after it and it was PSG's turn to experience that. They couldn't handle it.

They actually had an early chance, but their centre-forward put it wide and from there on in it was all us. Jamie had a shot that grazed the post after 10 minutes and that got the crowd baying even more and, after 12 minutes, that vital first breakthrough arrived and, naturally, it was Robbie who was on hand.

Collymore was having a good night and his presence was upsetting PSG. He managed to nod the ball down to Robbie who volleyed what was only really a half-chance, like a flash past Bernard Lama in goal. "Come on! Two more goals." The volume went up, but I remember Macca telling everyone to be calm. Steve always was very relaxed.

Collymore continued to run at the French as we continued to press forward. We looked comfortable at the back, but I did have to throw myself at a PSG shot that looked goalbound. It was going to be one of those nights. As we piled everything forward in hope, chances were bound to come on the breakaway.

YOU HAVE TO adapt to whom you are playing against, especially as a defender. I never cared who I was facing. You couldn't, otherwise you wouldn't sleep. I couldn't tell you who they had up front. It didn't mean a thing to me. They could have had Pele playing and it wouldn't have bothered me, he would have got kicked!

I was so up for it. Sometime later I had a Japanese club after me and I considered seeing out the end of my career out there like Lineker had done. My agent had a video of this match made to send them, but in the end I had to edit it because in the first half, the PSG centre-forward caught me late and as I got up I've called him an "'effing so and so." He's going on at me in French, which isn't my strong point, so rather than rowing I've discreetly given him the back of my hand. Well, the video caught this and I could hardly send one of me doing that.

THE SECOND HALF was played at an even higher tempo, made even more fervent as we were now attacking the Kop and PSG set their stall out to do nothing but defend. Jason McAteer had a decent chance and Collymore had a free kick well saved by Lama.

The clock was ticking and every time we swept towards the Kop a cheer went up that rocked the old stadium. We had been getting so close, we had chances cleared off the line and scrambles in the box, but it wouldn't go in.

My magic moment arrived with 11 minutes to go. I hit a 30-yard volley; I put a bit of bend on it and it flew into the top corner. Those fans who watched me play will know that's bullshit. Stig knocked a good corner in and I just went after it. I connected. Sometimes you just connect and I caught that right in the centre of my forehead and it went in like a bullet. I was so pleased. It was a great goal, but now we knew we had just ten minutes to get at them to score that all-important equalizer and we knew it would just be us attacking them defending.

We mullered them; pulverised them. Robbie hit an effort that shaved the post and they continued to clear chances away. I've never seen so many shots cleared off the line. It was corner after corner and chance after chance. Even David James came forward for a corner and actually got his head to the ball, but it shaved the crossbar.

WE WERE CONVINCED that we would do it. They had gone, their heads had gone. They were booting the ball out of play, just to win some time. If it had gone to extra time we would have beaten them, no doubt about it.

It wasn't to be. When the whistle went, the relief on their faces. My God! I was gobsmacked. I couldn't believe it. The Kop, though, were, as ever, brilliant.

They were fantastic supporters. They get disappointed by players and the greed that is prevalent in the game, but if they see the effort being put in they will cheer you on to the end. They really know their football up there and that night they knew we were so close and that we should have been through. We were gutted, but they clapped us off. It's nice to be appreciated, but it was no consolation at the time.

YOU HAD TO feel for Roy. I'm sure he must have looked at himself and how we played in Paris. Now I am in management that decision would definitely keep me up at night, but that's football.

The dressing room was quiet. We had lost a semi-final and it's a case of "What if?" What can you say? Ronnie Moran came around to each of us and just said, "You could have done no more than you did, son. Get your head up." That was typical Ronnie. He might have even said "well done" to me. That's a big deal for Ronnie that is.

It was a major disappointment, but with time I can look back fondly, not on the result but on the occasion. The atmosphere, the game, the goal, it all stands out for me. Sure, we didn't win through and sure there was ultimately no glory, but that kind of night and its emotion and passion was the reason I joined Liverpool.

I won the FA Cup and we played in big games, but this was a semi-final of a European competition and the whole night, the preparation, going out to the crowd, the buzz, the support, the noise, the flags; I had never seen too much of that and remember, I had played in the semi-final of the World Cup. It is a great memory and one I will always cherish. That was what Liverpool was all about for me, and to be part of a night like that meant everything. It still does.

GARY MCALLISTER: BORN 25 DECEMBER 1964, MOTHERWELL; 87 GAMES, 9 GOALS

Gary McAllister

Liverpool 5 CD Alavés 4
(Liverpool win on Golden Goal)

UEFA Cup Final

Wednesday 16 May 2001

IF YOU GREW up when I did or started playing football and pursuing it as a career when I did you couldn't help but admire Liverpool Football Club. We all admired Liverpool. You couldn't help but watch that team of the 1970s and 1980s and appreciate them. You didn't have to support them, but you could see that theirs were players worth looking up to.

I was a fan of football and so you had to admire them. The way they passed the ball and the way they dominated European football. I think you'll find that most of my generation had a soft spot for the club.

When I was breaking into the game as a boy, Graeme Souness was *the* man. He was at the forefront; he was everything that I felt a midfielder should be. He was the master and he was in a Liverpool shirt. And he was Scottish.

At the age of 36, I thought my time had passed. I'd had a good career, won the league with Leeds in 1992 and plenty of caps for Scotland, but suddenly here I was, lifting the third trophy of an amazing season, a major European honour and I'd been named Man of the Match. That night in Dortmund will always stay with me, because if I'm honest, at my time of life, it was all so unexpected.

We'd won the UEFA Cup and I looked into the crowd to see my wife with a beaming grin on her face. She had had such a tough year with her illness and had had to endure some serious treatment, but she had got there and that was special. We'd done it. We'd taken Liverpool's name back to the peaks of European football and had matched the occasions that I had grown up watching as an awe-inspired kid.

AS I SAY, I never thought it would happen, although for a long time my name had been linked with a move to the club. When Kenny Dalglish was manager he had made enquiries, as had Roy Evans. Kenny actually made a firm move for me when I was at Leeds and he was manager of Blackburn.

He was building his team at Ewood Park and wanted both David Batty and myself to make the move across the Pennines. I had worked all my life to get to a big club and felt I had made it at Leeds United. Blackburn were starting their revolution with Jack Walker's millions but I felt I didn't want to go back to what I saw as a club similar to Leicester. With hindsight I was a bit of a mug. David moved and won the Premiership there, whilst I stayed and watched Leeds' form dip.

I ended up at Coventry and had a great season in 2000. The cruciate ligament injury from a couple of seasons before was now fine and I was back playing well. I had said to myself that I haven't got long left here, so I should start enjoying it. At Coventry I had teamed up with Chippo, Hadji and Robbie Keane. Robbie was great for me. He inspired me in many ways with his enthusiasm. If you play with such a sharp frontman it can be a second wind for us old midfielders.

I got wind that Gérard Houllier and Liverpool were keen. My agent, Struan Marshall, who looked after a few of the Liverpool boys, told me there was some interest from the club and if they made the Champions League it would definitely happen. So of course, Liverpool lose their last game of 1999/00 at Bradford and are out of that and I'm thinking, "That's that knackered."

Gérard, though, remained interested and we arranged a meeting. We were about to start negotiations and Struan said he would go in alone. I made it clear that I was not going to miss out on this opportunity over money and that there should be no hard bargaining. No agent will say that his or her client will come for nothing, but at the time I would have. It all went very smoothly and I was, at last, a Liverpool player.

THE PASSING GAME is how I think football should be played. I think Gérard was looking for a player who could link the midfield with the attack, but who also had that bit more experience. He was concerned that he'd lost Steve McManaman, Paul Ince and Steve Staunton and so it was a very young squad he had there. I offered a bit of know-how. Not necessarily a player that the others would look up to, but he knew that I had always tried to train the way I play, with the right attitude. He made it clear that as much as I could offer on the Saturday, I could also benefit his team all week long. I was happy with that.

Of those young players, Steven Gerrard was beginning to stand out. He had made his debut the season before and now had become a regular in the midfield. I had played against him and, whilst today he is a man, back then he was a young foal. He was getting injured a lot because his body was developing, but instantly I knew there wasn't much I could teach Steven Gerrard.

He was and is fantastic, but I hope he picked up little bits from me. I'd like to think he did. I do think that midfield play gets better as you get older. As long as the legs can keep up with the brain that is. Look at Roy Keane, he is still a very good footballer. The key is realising when to make that run and also that standing still can benefit a team. Trying to get kids to stand still so that the ball will come to *them* is hard. They want to charge around looking for it. Stand still and watch play develop. Decision-making is vital and, as you get older, those decisions become easier. You don't have to make that killer pass every time, you have to be patient and it will happen for you. That advice is crucial.

You must also make sure at the same time that you don't take that enthusiasm away from a young player. If he wants to play that long pass then you must let him know there is a right time for it and it can be a great weapon. I think Stevie's game has taken all that on board and he has taken a lot from watching maybe a few older midfield players. The simple pass can also be the best pass.

WHEN I ARRIVED at Liverpool, I was immediately struck by Gérard Houllier and how intent he was on bringing success to a club that he genuinely loved. His chats in pre-season were really centred on finding out from us players where we saw the club going. He would get us to write down in private where we saw ourselves finishing in the league and how far we could go in cups. A few took the piss and put "Staying up!", but all in all we were on the same wavelength.

Within the dressing room we all felt that we could win a cup. We sensed that there were good enough players to go and win something. There were other teams ahead of us in terms of winning the championship, but Liverpool must always be capable of competing with the best and challenging for honours. The fans demand that.

I had a good feeling about it. I had to watch the negative things. "Why the fuck are we signing a 36-year-old?" asked the editor of one of the club's big fanzines. So I obviously had to prove that I could do the job.

I had always loved playing at Anfield as a visitor. The "THIS IS ANFIELD" sign, the fans, the great pitch. I always loved it. It's just a great arena. I was an opposing player and then I became one of them and I never tired of the place. Even today. I went to the Champions League semi-final against Chelsea and I have never seen anything like that. The place to be is Chelsea at the moment with all the cash enticing the greatest players on the planet to West London, but Chelsea could never, ever host a night like they witnessed at Anfield. It doesn't matter how much money is injected, they could never recreate the passion of that cauldron and that's what makes Anfield extra special.

Houllier had seen that, he knew about the place and its history and, as I say, was desperate to recreate those famous victories that the other lads in this book were all part of setting down in history. I spoke to him a lot. Gérard was very diligent. His organisation was incredible and he knew exactly what he wanted from certain parts of the team. The defence was drilled, the midfield, the attack, they were three parts of a whole.

IF YOU WERE to make one criticism of Gérard it was that he needed to be a wee bit more free if he wanted to win the Premiership. The set-up meant that we were made for cup competitions. We had young Michael Owen up front and on a given day he could win a game with just a half-chance.

Liverpool were criticised under Gérard for the counter-attacking style of play, but it could win us matches. I did feel, though, that we needed to open up a bit if we were going to win the league. You have to have the attitude that if the opposition score two, we'll score three. That outlook wins titles.

He was very precise, very measured. You did your job, in your part of the pitch. Be careful; don't get caught in case they break. I was used as a more defensive midfield player whilst my mind-set was to get forward and support the attack. In our team the two wide men were the more offensive of the midfielders. The two central guys were asked to sit back. It worked though. I was there for two seasons, from 2000 to 2002, where we really didn't lose too many games.

Manchester United couldn't beat us. Houllier had the upper hand over Fergie for a bit, but all the same, United were winning leagues. That was because they opened up that bit more. United wanted to get their front men playing, with Sheringham dropping deep and dictating the play. They couldn't get that going against us. Didi Hamann would do a job on them and block those channels. My point is that I just think that we needed to take a few more risks and that team, who had some wonderful footballers, could have taken the Premiership. If we could have found a middle ground between the expansive stuff that was played under Roy Evans and the more measured play under Gérard then we could have done it, I have no doubt about that.

Saying that, we finished second in 2002 with 80 points, enough to win the League in many seasons. Arsenal went and won their last 13 games to finish with 87 points and that kind of run is scary. So Gérard was very close to bringing the title to Liverpool and I really enjoyed playing there and the way it was run. The Spice Boy thing had been eradicated by a very strict regime brought in by Gérard. He got a grip at the training ground, the timekeeping, and the dress codes. It was like being back at primary school. Mobile phones were to be kept off; when we travelled everyone wore the same club tracksuit or suit. When we had breakfast, it was in red tops and blue bottoms. Lunch was white tops and so on. The schedules were printed out and passed around. Train, eat, sleep, call your wife, it was all given a time. Some people would say that's childish, but the point is if you get that into your routine it makes you much more disciplined when the game starts.

THAT WAS BEGINNING to show with our team and in February we won the League Cup against Birmingham. We were in the quarter-finals of the UEFA Cup, still going well in third place in the Premiership and making good ground in the FA Cup. Trebles were never mentioned, but we were getting some attention and felt that we could use the momentum that we were building up to our advantage.

Games were coming thick and fast, but it was in Europe that Gérard used me most regularly. It was not as fierce. If we were approaching a European match, Gérard would pull me aside on the Saturday and say, "I'm leaving you out, but you'll be in on Thursday night." When I signed I knew I would be used, not sparingly, but certainly not in every game. I'm from the old school, though, and wanted to play every game, but the way it worked out was perfect.

I had given up my international career and so I loved that UEFA Cup run. It had that international feel to it and I was playing good players that you didn't face week-in week-out. That turned me on. You knew you had to be on your game because you were competing with some of the best around.

Liverpool in Europe is so special. The flags, the songs, the banners, the way the fans have got to games, there is something different about the way the Liverpool fans do it. You see the well-dressed guys who jet out to away games and then you see some blokes who probably walked it or hitched there. I had watched Liverpool over the years in Europe and always had wanted to be a part of one of these nights.

I got one when we went out to Rome to face Roma in the famous stadium in which the club had won the European Cup in 1977 and 1984. You can't help but feel close to the guys that won those games and now you're following in their footsteps. OK, it wasn't a final and it was the UEFA Cup, but that 2-0 win in Rome meant as much to us. It will go down as one of the great Liverpool away performances in Europe.

The second leg was nothing less than bloody scary. I don't know what happened there. We're 1-0 down and they have shouted for a late penalty and the ref's given it. Straight away there are one or two of us in his ear. "It was never a penalty." Carra, myself, we were giving the ref an almighty load of abuse. The Roma player is picking up the ball, turns around and the ref's now pointing to the corner flag. Oh my God! They were going mental afterwards. You can imagine, there was mayhem. A lot of Italian melodrama. I don't know what made the referee change his mind, but I'm mighty glad that he did.

THE PORTO GAME in the next round was a dull affair. I was sub for both games, but the first leg will be remembered because not one thing happened in the whole game. There were 70,000 people and you could have heard a pin drop. There wasn't a shot in 90 minutes. 0-0 was a brilliant result for us, though, and we easily beat them back at Anfield.

In the semi-final we faced Barcelona and we were all well up for playing in the Nou Camp. I had played there before for Leeds, but you never get used to playing in a stadium like that. Again, Gérard took a lot of abuse from them because we battled to a 0-0 draw and they said he had "Murdered Football".

What did they expect? If we had gone to the Nou Camp and played an open game on that massive pitch we would have been the ones murdered. We weren't there to make them look good. Michael played up on his own and we had five across the middle. They hated it. Jari Litmanen had arrived at Liverpool and he had been out there. He bought the Catalan sports paper and he translated it telling us how much stick we and the manager were getting. When you look at the club now it seems strange that we needed a Finn to translate our Spanish.

Gérard loved it. The De Boers were giving it plenty, saying that we would have to come out and play at Anfield and then they would smash us. Rivaldo made a few comments too, but it just spurred Gérard on.

The second leg was amazing. I remember we were waiting to kick off and we all just looked at each other, and the noise, bloody hell. It was similar to the night I played at Ibrox with Leeds and they had banned the Leeds fans. It was so loud.

It was buzzing. We got a penalty and, by now, it was me who was taking them. Michael had missed one against Roma and so I inherited them and was scoring a few. I missed that famous one in Euro 1996, but from there to 2002 I think I missed only one.

Against Barcelona, I put the ball down and the goal looked tiny. Pepe Reina, Liverpool's keeper today, was in goal and was making himself look very big and I believe he has a very good record with penalties. I was always going to the keeper's right, but fortunately I managed to stick it right in the postage stamp, where the post meets the crossbar. Let's just say I meant to be that precise.

I remember placing the ball and Puyol, their defender was in my ear trying to put me off. When I scored I was so elated that I went over to him and punched the air right in front of his face. Steven Gerrard had run over to me and I caught him smack in the face with the follow through!

We'd been desperate to score first because if they'd managed to, they could shut up shop, but the key from here on was the way we kept possession. If you give a team like Barcelona the ball they'll make you suffer. They proved that when they came back the following season in the Champions League and they gave us the run around. They were playing football as good as anyone in the world at the time and so to play like we did in that semi-final was special. The 1-0 win saw us through to the final.

The De Boers and others went on about how they were the best side over the two legs, but we were in the final, not them, so who cares? We didn't. You could forgive the De Boers. They come from a very arrogant footballing race who think that their way of playing football is the only way.

THE OTHER SEMI had been between Alavés and the German side Kaiserslautern. We knew even before the Barcelona result that if we won we would be favourites. We had the tradition, the history in Europe and whilst the Spaniards had a great team that season, we were the high profile club. We were favourites, but had got used to being underdogs for most of our journey to the final.

You look at that trophy and there are not many minnows' names on it. There is something in tradition and clubs who have that legacy often do well because they carry their name into matches. We did that. Liverpool have that tradition and when faced with Alavés, no disrespect, but we had that extra thing about us.

The closer you get to the final, they start bringing out all the old photos and showing the goals on the telly. You begin to think, I want a bit of that. That drives you on. The opposition would have been aware of our history and that can put them on the back foot.

I was really enjoying my football and I went on a run of games where I couldn't stop scoring. As well as the Barcelona game I scored free kicks against Coventry and Bradford, a penalty against Tottenham and of course the free kick that beat Everton at Goodison. That was a crazy one. When that went in you start allowing yourself to think the season was destined to be a great one.

Gérard was chopping and changing and that squad rotation was working. He was trying to juggle it all and come the FA Cup final at Cardiff against Arsenal it was hard to know who would be in. I was on this run of scoring goals and was desperate to be involved. I had played in the Barcelona semi-final, but I felt that was my European final. Now I wanted to be involved in the FA Cup showpiece.

He named the team and I was not in it. He called me to his hotel room to explain his decision, but I wasn't up for his explanations. I said, "Listen, I'm focused. I'm not going to act like a kid, I'm not going to sulk, but I'm not happy. We'll speak about this later."

Anyway, I got on and set up our equaliser and we won 2-1. Michael was amazing. During the course of the brief celebrations in Wales, Gérard gave me the nod as if to say, "You're in for the UEFA Cup game, son." It sounds like a master plan doesn't it? "I'll bring you on when we're 1-0 down in the FA Cup final, we'll win that and then you'll play a big part in the Alavés game." Anyway, I got that wink and from there my mind was on the final.

WE'D WON THE FA Cup, but we could hardly let our hair down. We knew we had another Cup final in three or four days' time. It was a hungry squad. I had won the league in the past, but was desperate to win more and I don't think anyone else in that squad had won any major honours. The League Cup had been won before by the likes of Fowler and of course we had won it only months before, but FA Cups, UEFA Cups, a chance to play in the Champions League, these were a big deal and we all wanted to achieve the same things.

That discipline that I mentioned earlier meant we would eat together, train, meet to catch a plane. It was all regimented, but it had to be. We'd won the FA Cup, but now it was on to the next one.

The thing that I enjoyed about it was that I was supposed to be winding down my career. I felt like I was a young man again in a major tournament with my country. When you go to World Cups it's intense. You have four weeks' preparation, then you're travelling, living and playing together. It had that feel about it and I loved that. There's nothing more special to me than my family, but I love being involved in football and I miss it when I'm not doing it. Football has been my life; it's what I know, so that week for Liverpool was something special.

I enjoyed the fact that it was just a case of running into the house, packing another bag and then you're away again. We've just won the cup at the Millennium Stadium, my first FA Cup and then we're off to Europe for another final. It was magic.

WE DIDN'T KNOW much about Alavés, but they had had a fine season in La Liga. There weren't many household names, but by the time it came to the match, we knew each and every one of them. Javi Moreno had been scoring goals for fun in Spain and Europe. Jordi Cruyff, of course, had been at Manchester United. Gérard knew that night it was more about us than them and this was an occasion when the shackles could come off a wee bit.

We came out at a frightening pace and began to open them up. I thought, "This is going to be five or six-nil". I really did because they didn't know what had hit them. That's how quickly we started.

I think we surprised them. In fact I think we surprised everyone. I knocked in a free kick in the opening minutes and Markus Babbel headed us in front. We looked good. Didi and myself were sitting in the middle whilst Stevie Gerrard was racing up and down on the right wing. He didn't want to do it. That wasn't his natural game, but someone had to and it was clear that I couldn't. My legs wouldn't have allowed that.

Stevie was always going to be able to get forward from there. That's where I see Steve's game. Not out wide, but I like him having the freedom to roam. People think he's a Souness, dictating things and holding a position on the halfway line. I don't. Steve's at his best going forward and that night he could do that.

He got his goal, our second, by running through from the inside-right position and buried it past Herrera in the Alavés goal. While we celebrated you could see the whites of their eyes. They were a shambles. I'm thinking, "This is going to be easy." But then their manager, Jose Manuel Esnal, brought on Ivan Alonso, a Uruguayan, up front who was very good in the air and he started causing Stephane Henchoz tremendous problems.

TACTICALLY IT WAS a strange game. We'd scored twice, but they pulled one back and then we got another, but throughout it, the Alavés coach was changing formations, changing tactics and that was very brave. He was going for broke. It can't have been too easy at 2-0 down, but their manager just went very offensive and it caught out our guys at the back.

Ivan Alonso beat Markus Babbel to the ball to make it 2-1 and suddenly we had a game on our hands again. Contra was a fine right-back and was getting forward a lot. He crossed a dangerous ball again, but this time Sander Westerveld saved from Moreno.

With half-time approaching we managed to gather our senses and we picked them off again. Didi played a lovely pass through to Michael to run on to. He knocked it past Herrera and was brought down. Penalty. No doubt about it. The goalkeeper had to go. Surely.

You don't want to see people sent off, but those are the rules and we were screaming that he should be sent off. That would surely have been that then.

But the ref didn't red card the Spanish keeper. He kept him on. Which meant now I was facing him with the penalty.

I'd actually got Euro 96 out of my system very quickly. Scotland had a game the following June in Belarus and it was one of those World Cup qualifiers at the end of a season when the pitch is a cabbage patch and it was 0-0 with not long left. I took the penalty and managed to score. That erased any doubts in my mind, although they may never leave the Tartan Army.

Against Alavés I took a decent one, but on my run up I slipped a wee bit and, whilst the keeper got a hand on it, the power I generated saw it home. As the whistle blew we had that two-goal cushion again, but you knew there was still a lot to do. You really did. "Not so easy any more," I now thought.

GÉRARD WOULD NEVER get carried away. We had knocked them back with my goal, but were aware that the next goal was vital. Gérard told us that we had done well, but now there was no need to go chasing the game. We had that two-goal cushion and that our natural instinct should be to sit on it.

That, though, so nearly proved our downfall. I'm not bullshitting; even then I thought, "This could be dangerous. If we sit back here we could be punished." If we had gone out and started the second half the way we had set about them in the first, game over. Instead we were a wee bit too cautious. We got into two lines of four with one of the forwards drifting back to help to make a midfield five. When we did get the ball we were all 80 yards away from the goal and that became a problem as, when we lost possession they were already in our half.

So I was no surprise when, in the 48th minute, Moreno scored a good header to underline how good a player he was. Three minutes later they won a free kick out side of our box and it was vital that we try and see out this spell of pressure.

As a wall we used to always jump. If Moreno had done his homework and seen that and purposefully tried to put it under us then he's a bloody genius but I think he miskicked it and it's caught Sander flat footed. 3-3. "Bollocks"

Then we started playing again. How nice was it, though, to be able to bring on someone like Robbie Fowler. Someone hungry and someone fresh. That was the beauty of that squad.

Robbie was something else. I had played against him loads of times and his eye for goal was like nothing I'd ever seen. Awesome. The injuries took their toll and that was very cruel on him. He's a clever lad Robbie. I know he got this reputation for fooling around, but he was switched on and I'll tell you what else, he loved that club with the passion of a schoolboy.

He had that cheekiness about him. I remember in the final that I went over to take a corner in front of our fans. The Liverpool subs were warming up and as I'm putting the ball into the quadrant a huge dildo comes flying on to the pitch next to us. Robbie went over to it, flicked it up and volleyed it back into the crowd. I was in hysterics. The lads must have been doing a bit of shopping in the more adult of Dortmund shops. Typical Robbie, though. Most would have shied away from that, but he had to have the last laugh. Brilliant.

The injuries had meant that he couldn't get back the form that saw him bag over a century of goals for the club, but still he could offer so much. Great to play with and to link with, but when it came to natural finishing no one was like him. Left foot, right foot, good in the air. Michael Owen was a goalscorer and wouldn't stop scoring. Robbie felt he should have been starting a bit more, but Gérard had hard decisions to make. I'm sure Robbie was gutted to again miss out on the starting XI for that final. I was too interested in my own routine to notice, but he's a great pro and he's come on and got us a goal. For all we knew, the winning goal coming with less than 20 minutes to go. What more can you ask for? His strike was awesome. He took the ball, drifted and feinted to shoot, made space and knocked it in with his weaker right foot.

WE WERE BACK on top. What a roller-coaster night. The crowd were amazing. The fans hadn't stopped singing. You're expecting the crowd to be half and half, but this was so in our favour. We had threequarters of the place. I wish I had written down some of the slogans on the banners. It was the same in Turkey, I'm told. Those fans were great. The humour is always there. I associate big European nights with Liverpool and now I was involved in my own and it looked like we had pulled off a famous win.

In the last minute, though, disaster. We let them back in. It was sickening. It was a great set piece for them to be fair, but we should have had someone charging at Jordi who shot, but we didn't. The ball ends up in our net and we suddenly have to go again.

Picking yourself up when you've conceded a late equaliser like that is never easy. You think it's not going to be your night and all the "what ifs?" race through your mind. Going into extra time the crowd were going nuts, they were making so much noise and whilst the situation was nerve-wracking and emotional, I didn't want it to end. I was loving every minute of it. It was an incredible experience. I felt so good. We had to push on, the onus was still on us. They had scored late and you would have expected them to have the ascendancy, but they had gone. They were desperate for penalties and that meant we could go for it.

As they tired, Alavés threw in reckless challenges; suddenly they were down to ten men with Magno sent off for a second yellow. Now they were defending for their lives, whilst we had fresh attacking legs on in Vladimir Smicer and Patrick Berger backing up Robbie. As time went on, though, it looked more and more like penalties and then it doesn't matter how many players the other team have got. It becomes much more of a lottery; it's anyone's game. So we had to make our numerical advantage count. Try as we might we couldn't break them down and so we were desperately throwing everything at them.

Their defending was equally desperate. Vlad was brought down by a terrible tackle with three minutes left and we knew that now was the time to score otherwise this was going into the lottery of penalties. The free kick was out on our left wing and I liked taking them from out there because you can whip them into the box at pace.

The way I did it was to try and aim for the far post and if it eludes everyone then it may just fly straight in. I saw it like a golf shot where I would be aiming for a line and hope someone nods it goalwards, but if they don't then it might just go in anyway.

We had big Sami, Didi, and Stevie up there. All big guys and I just wanted to get it in at pace and make Alavés defend it. I whipped it in, it evaded the first two jumpers and their defender, Geli, got a faint nick on it and the next thing I know it's hit the back of the net. I swear that it would have gone in anyway to be honest, but that was that, we'd won.

I was away, I was off celebrating MY goal! It was pandemonium, there were bodies all over me, the subs, the bench, the backroom, they were all on top of me. The funny thing was, though, that there were a couple of the lads who still thought we had a few minutes defending to do. I'm sure Didi Hamann was one of them, he was making his way back to our half not realising it was the golden goal. He was looking over as if to say, "Bloody hell, stop celebrating. Get back here and defend!"

It was a great moment and I felt so happy for Gérard Houllier. That was the one he wanted. He had spent a lot of time working for UEFA and he had many of his former colleagues there. It meant a lot to him. He had earned his right to be regarded a European winner.

WE SAW ALAN Hansen afterwards and he said that he'd been going nuts in the BBC box. I was at the Liverpool v Chelsea game and all the ex-players were there. It's funny, I was only there a short time, but once you've been at that club it sucks you in. More so than any other. I love Leeds United and cherish the time and the players I worked with, but Liverpool grips you. Alan was jumping about like a lunatic against Alavés and we all were against Chelsea.

I was made Man of the Match and received my award from Johan Cruyff, which, of course, meant a lot. I had swapped shirts with his son Jordi Cruyff and went up to get my trophy before the main presentation. They wanted me in a Liverpool shirt though and I could hardly go and get the award from Johan with "Cruyff" on my back. I had to steal Nick Barmby's shirt off him for my big moment. I've got a lot of photos of that presentation and I've got "Barmby" on my back. It was great for me, having grown up admiring Cruyff and now he's giving me an award for the Man of the Match in a major European final. It was dream stuff.

Robbie and Sami lifted the trophy together. It's beautiful. It's not as nice as that one with big ears they won in Istanbul, but I suppose if I want to see that one now I just have to pop up to Anfield. It's there for keeps, after all.

That game, that night, those fans; it was perfect. The only downside was that we were straight on the plane afterwards and heading to London for Saturday's match with Charlton. Yes we still had one league game to play.

That was the sort of season it was, though. We achieved so much and the fans were with us every step of the way. Some were at The Valley in the same clothes as they had worn at Cardiff the week before. They had gone from Wales to Dortmund and now they were in London. They didn't look like they'd slept much either.

THAT EXPERIENCE HELPED Carra, Steve, and Sami in their quest for the Champions League. They learnt how to play against quality opposition and how to defend when you're under the cosh. They had to learn all that in 2001 and you could see that they had taken that into their incredible run in the Champions League.

What we achieved was fantastic and it meant the world to me, in the context of the club's history it wasn't their best achievement, but in the context of my career it's right up there.

I very rarely keep photos of my career and if I do they hardly ever go up on the wall. At the top of my house there's a flight of stairs that takes you to the kiddies' rooms and that is lined with my pictures. seventy-five per cent of those are from the Alavés game. That's how much the occasion means to me.

JAMIE CARRAGHER: BORN 28 JANUARY 1978, LIVERPOOL; 366 GAMES, 3 GOALS

Jamie Carragher

Liverpool 3 AC Milan 3
(Liverpool win 3-2 on penalties)

UEFA Champions' League Final

Wednesday 25 May 2005

THE ROOM WAS quiet. Nothing was being said. Nothing could be said. We were 3-0 down in the biggest game of our lives. We were getting beat; make that getting slaughtered and, for now, what could any of us say? The only noise was the manager working away on the board trying to rectify the team and its tactics.

Suddenly, through the silence you could hear You'll Never Walk Alone as our fans incredibly found their voice once more. I'd like to say that it inspired me and made want to go out and claw the three goals back, made us turn in the performance of our lives to pull off that incredible comeback; but if I'm honest it just made me feel that much worse. "They're doing their bit, but we haven't done ours," I thought. I was gutted. I felt like crying for them at that point.

They were singing away despite thinking that they were going to lose. I spoke to some after and the odd one was like, "I knew we were going to win", but I don't believe that for a minute. I certainly didn't think we could do it. But we did and what a night. What a crazy, unforgettable, amazing night.

It's got to go down in history as one of the best-ever finals. People rightly go on about the 1960 game between Real Madrid and Eintracht Frankfurt and I think that the night in Istanbul will be the same. In 20, no 30 years time people will still be talking about what was an incredible match. I have got about seven or eight years left of my career and I think if I am going to ever top that I'll have to play in a World Cup final and score a hat-trick!

WATCHING US OVER the season you would never have thought that we could have created such excitement. Our league form had suffered badly as we progressed through Europe. Some of our players were better suited for the Champions League matches because, and this doesn't sound a nice thing to say about your own team-mates, it was less of a battle.

It's a totally different game in Europe, a different pace with different referees who look at things in a different way to our own officials. We'd change our tactics in Europe, but that was down to circumstance more than anything. Fernando Morientes was cup-tied and Djibril Cissé had that hideous broken leg, so we had to play with Milan Baros alone up there and that made us stronger defensively.

Look at Louis Garcia. He seemed far more suited to Europe and he actually managed to score five or six very important goals for us. He was afforded more time and that suits Louis who is still getting used to the rough and tumble of the Premiership.

Looking back you can cite the Olympiakos game as the night we started to approach the Champions League with real belief. Things like that win over the Greeks happen for a reason and the way we came back from two goals down to get the winner with four minutes left gave us such belief. I'm sure if you ask the guys who played against St Etienne in 1977 they'd say that after that win they felt that this had to be their year. It was meant to be and that was the same for us after Olympiakos. You just felt that this was the prelude to something special.

But we hadn't seen anything yet. The Chelsea match was just one of the best. It was a privilege to not only be playing, but just to be in the ground. Usually when the game's being played it's hard to know what's going on in the stands, but we went out to warm up about half an hour before kick off and all the old songs were being sung and you knew, you knew this was something different. I knew it was going to be a big occasion because our fans rise to those sort of matches, but I also think that us scoring so early added to the passion.

Had Chelsea scored within five minutes it might have killed the crowd and then of course we had the six minutes of added time at the end where each person was on the edge of their seats. Scarves were being waved around everyone's heads and I remember thinking to myself this is like being in front of a South American set of fans. I've seen Boca Juniors on the television and that is what it is like. The energy was incredible.

I'VE PLAYED IN a few great atmospheres, the night that Gérard Houllier came back from his illness against Roma in 2002 was one and, of course, being local boys, Stevie Gerrard and myself have grown up hearing about Inter Milan and St Etienne. To hear that those who sampled those nights as players thought that they were matched by that Chelsea night is fantastic.

Not that it wasn't without its scares. Eidur Gudjohnsen had a real chance at the end. Jerzy went for a cross and missed it and then life became slow motion. Gudjohnsen shot and the fact that I never touched it into the net myself was unbelievable. I never knew where Drogba was and I just turned, thinking that the ball would be nestling in the net. Just thinking about it now sickens me, it really does. Imagine if we had got that close? There would have been no coming back then. I just lay there on the floor for about ten seconds and looked up at the sky feeling nothing but sheer relief.

The euphoria at the final whistle of that game basically continued until Paulo Maldini scored in the first minute of the final. The Chelsea win had brought such a sense of triumph to the city and to our fans who were convinced we were going to win the European Cup. As our run to the final had been so memorable, we travelled with all the fans' optimism.

I watch a lot of European football, though, and knew how good this team we were facing could be. A lot of our fans may have watched the second leg against PSV and thought that Milan might be a pushover. You only had to ask Manchester United's players and fans to know how special Milan could be. They had battered United, they really were brilliant. I knew we would find the final tough.

Try telling the fans that though. They were on a crest of a wave after the semi and who could blame them. What they had nicely chosen to ignore was how bad we'd been in the league. I went to

Turkey thinking it was going to be a really tight game, but one in which we could nick something. We'd done that against other teams on the way to Istanbul and if we could stay defensively strong, then we had the ability to score a goal to nick the game. I had a chat with Stevie the night before and we both agreed that it would be 1-0 either way. There wasn't going to be many goals.

A few of us had been involved in the UEFA Cup final in 2001 and we knew the key was to approach the game like any other. That, though, is easier said than done. In fact it becomes impossible. People are ringing and texting you non-stop wishing you luck, there's a mad clamour for tickets, and the buzz is almost unbearable.

WE FLEW OUT two days before the match and the hotel was chocker with UEFA officials, ex-players, celebrities and press. It was as if the whole of Europe had descended on Istanbul for that one match. It began to sink in just how big this game was.

Rafa wanted to try and keep things as normal as possible, but he knew he was fighting a losing battle. The only thing different from the management's point of view was that we travelled two days before the game rather than the day before.

It was probably a good thing, getting us out of Liverpool. The atmosphere in the city was nuts with expectation. The local papers ran nothing but stories on the match so it was quite a relief to leave and get away from all the hype.

I wasn't nervous, I'm not the type. I was more excited than anything. I'm about to play in a European Cup final and I just wanted to get started. I slept fine the night before, no problem. I had another kip in the afternoon. I never struggle sleeping. The game was on my mind though. Who would I be up against? How would the game go? You play the match in your head. I usually score the winner in those. In my head I wasn't worrying about them. I wanted to start the game well, get a few good touches early on; some good passes and relax into it. Ease in.

We couldn't have been better prepared. We had ten days between our last Premiership game and the final and so every day we were working on one thing, playing against AC Milan. We were recreating possible scenarios. How do we play if we are winning 1-0 with ten minutes to go, how do we play if we are 1-0 down with ten minutes to go. Rafa's good, but even he didn't practise what we should do if we are 3-0 down at half-time!

We were all in the dark about the team the manager would pick, but I'd pretty much guessed a few days before hand to be honest. I could work it out by the teams he was playing in training. Steve was being used in midfield a lot rather than off the strikers and so I realised that Harry might have a chance. Having said that, I thought Djibril Cissé would start, so I'm not as good a sleuth as I thought.

He didn't actually tell us the team until an hour and a half before kick off. It was quite a shock to everyone because it wasn't how we'd played prior to the final, but as soon as it's named you have to get on with things.

The dressing room was quiet, it always is before games. We don't have many shouters in the team and everyone looks after themselves. To be honest you're just making sure you're alright. Once the team is named I'm always first on the massage table. I usually hop up on that and relax with the programme. It's difficult, though, when it's in Turkish.

For the Champions League games you have to be there an hour and a half before kick off whereas it can be an hour back home. That leaves a lot of time on our hands so we went out on to the pitch.

We knew how much money some of the fans had spent to get here and as we went out we thought, bloody hell there's more than the 30,000 everyone talked about here. The banners were all there. I loved them. Some of them even had my name on. God, that made me feel good. Every coach, every bus had something. I knew from my own family and mates how much the tickets were costing some. You were talking £1,000 and that's before you add the ale money.

The fans were a big part of the manager's final team talk and he mentioned just how many had made the trip and that we had to do it for them. He talked about the contrast between the number of Milan fans and our own. It was three or four to one and that showed how much we mean to them.

Tactically, Rafa wanted to get at Milan, that was key. He'd studied videos and seen the damage that PSV had done to them in the semi-final and so that's how he hoped it would go. That's why he named the team he did. He was picking a team to win.

WE GOT OUT there and were all well focused. I felt good. We kicked off and then boom, we're losing. It was our kick off! How did they score a goal from our bloody kick off? Djimi Traore was a bit nervous and he lost the ball and then gave away a foul. From that free kick they scored. We had built up for this for ten days, and then within a minute we were 1-0 down. You might as well as be in a second leg of a tie, and a goal down. None of us had had a kick and it's killed everything. The game plan, the atmosphere, it's all gone.

Mind you, for the next ten or fifteen minutes we played well and created chances. We were passing the ball well. John Arne Riise had a good shot, Sami had a good header, Luis had some half chances. It was going OK. We always wanted the ball, the full-backs were getting forward and we were going after the game. That, though, was to prove costly. As we went up the pitch, defending high, they could pick us off on the break. And, of course, they did.

Personally I felt good. After the goal, I had some good touches of the ball, was passing well and felt switched on. There was no time to be nervous. My whole mind was on trying to get us back into the game.

Soon though, the manager had more to think about. Not only were we a goal down, but now Harry Kewell was clearly struggling and would have to come off. It was all going wrong out there. As Harry limped off there were some boos from the fans and that was tough. I can understand the fans' response. They weren't booing because he was limping off in a European Cup final. Anyone with a brain would know he was never going to fake that. I think it was a culmination of things. Fans hadn't been happy with him since he arrived, rightly or wrongly. He'd snapped his groin though. You had to feel for him. He's playing in a European Cup final, you do your groin and the next day you're having an operation. He wasn't feigning injury I can tell you. After we'd won he was singing and dancing like us all, but a few days later I'm sure he was flat out. Having said that I bet he'd rather have that medal than have played the whole game and we'd lost.

Replacing Harry was Vladi Smicer. It was a surprise to us that Vlad came on. I thought that Didi would be the replacement, but at only 1-0 Rafa wanted to keep his original shape. Vlad went on to the right and Luis played off Baros. It was to be an incredible night for Vlad, in what was his last game for the club. He was very worried before the game. For our last Premiership match against Aston Villa, he hadn't even made the sixteen. Luckily for the Champions League you get a few more substitutes on the bench and now he was in.

We were holding our own, but at times were looking shaky. Djimi Traore was still a bit nervous and needed talking to. To be fair to him, to recover from the own goal he had scored against Burnley which knocked us out of the FA Cup back in January to win selection for a European final takes some doing. I needed to have the odd chat with him, though, because Milan were getting past him. We needed to hold a stronger line. He switched on and was immense in the second half.

His confidence had been knocked by the goal and he was having to make split-second decisions against a player like Andriy Shevchenko. He was playing them onside by dropping deep too much, but, as I say, these are split-second decisions and Djimi had to make them. I shouted at him, but I was just saying that we had to defend together. He was defending as an individual and we had to become one rather than four.

We had our moments and Luis looked to have been fouled for what we thought was a penalty to us, but there was no time to dwell on it because the game hadn't stopped and suddenly you've got Kaka, Shevchenko and Hernan Crespo running at you. It was an amazing break. Kaka put Shevchenko in and he crossed it past me for Crespo to score. I was lying on the turf thinking "2-0, that's it." At 1-0 I thought, "We're doing OK here, we might even get back in this", but 2-0 in a European Cup final, "This is going to be difficult."

DIFFICULT WAS ABOUT to turn into nigh on impossible. Kaka played through a brilliant pass which I stretched for, but couldn't intercept. At the time I thought, "Oh shit, I've made a mistake there", but I've watched it back and realise it was just a class ball. I wasn't sure whether I could have stayed on my feet and got it, but it's such a great pass there was nothing I could do. Crespo's finish was incredible and at 3-0 it's a rout.

Now I was just embarrassed. When you watch finals, no matter how big the gulf between the teams, they are always tight. You don't go 3-0 down before half-time in a European Cup final. It's not done. And I was just gutted. I thought about my mates who had come as fans, spent a load of money and, when the whistle went for the end of the half, I couldn't get in the dressing room quick enough.

If someone had said to me then, "This'll finish 3-0", I would have taken it. That sounds mad now that we won, but at the time I just wanted to stop the rot. I really was thinking that this could finish six.

We were devastated. A lot was made of Milan players singing victory songs at half-time, but I never heard any of that. Even if they were, you couldn't blame them, I think that's exactly what I would have been doing. They were about to win the European Cup. I think there was too much class in that Milan team, though, to start singing and dancing and I certainly didn't hear them.

The manager was calm. There was no big talk or anything. He just got on with sorting out the tactics and said, "Let's try and get the first goal". He was worried that Andrea Pirlo was controlling the game and by pushing Garcia and Gerrard forward they could stop him having so much of the ball. To be honest, I think he shared our worries that this could be five or six.

He was all set to bring Djimi off. He hadn't had the best of games, although he'd been better towards the end of the half. Djimi was all undressed and ready to get in the shower when Steve Finnan said his knee was sore and so Djimi's had to get dressed again, get his boots on and get ready to play another half.

We got out there, but again looked shaky and I remember Jerzy let an easy ball ricochet off his knees for a needless corner. I gave him a talking to for that one. I'll bollock anyone. It doesn't bother me. The most important thing is the football match, it doesn't matter if you lose friends now and then, the most important thing is to win. Jerzy is fine though. He takes it all.

He made amends with a fantastic save from a Shevchenko free-kick and then Xabi Alonso had a good shot go just wide. The fans were lifted slightly, but it wasn't as if we'd piled on the pressure. After half-time if anyone was going to score it was going to be them again. It wasn't like we came out flying.

But then we did score.

Stevie's goal didn't have me celebrating. I calmly made my way back into position hoping that it had stopped the rot. That goal only gave us a bit of relief. At least we'd scored; it lessened the embarrassment. The fans started to sing a few songs and it got everyone out of the doldrums a little bit. Maybe in hindsight it just brought the Milan players down a bit.

They'd blown it the year before in the quarter-final against La Coruna after being 4-1 up from the home leg and PSV had come so close to beating them in the semi-final, so in their minds there must have been a niggling worry. If you look at their performance in the second half it would suggest that they lost it. We were good, but they were bad. For six or seven minutes they seemed so dazed. Their manager, Carlo Ancelotti, later called it "six minutes of madness". Milan weren't tackling us, we started to have a lot of the ball and we went from there.

I WAS SEEING a lot of the ball. We had three on two at the back so one of us could step out and being behind we had nothing to lose. I went for it and found myself getting up in their half. Now I could sense their fear.

When Vlad picked up the ball and banged it in our growing hunger for the job in hand became real belief and their nerves became sheer dread. It was a great strike by Vlad, but the keeper might have a few doubts about himself there. They were screaming for offside, but the ref's just played an advantage because they had the ball, that was all. They gave it away and Vlad cracked a shot just inside the post. 3-2.

They shit themselves then. We were right back in it. I still didn't celebrate, I was urging us all on and from that moment each and every one of us wanted the ball, we were all so up for it and you couldn't help but feel that that we were going to get that third goal.

I surged forward again and played the ball into Milan Baros, who touched it in to Stevie. Milan didn't get the credit for that touch; it was great. He just nudged it round the corner and Steve's clear; flying towards goal. If that had been Bergkamp or someone like that they would have been raving, but Milan isn't known for that sort of play and it went unnoticed. I thought that was unfair.

You knew it was going to be a penalty because Steve's run was taking him across the defender and he's obviously going to be fouled. I still think Gattuso should have been sent off, mind. He was the last man. They said that Cafu was coming around to cover, but that was nonsense, he should have walked.

I followed up my forward momentum and ran into the penalty box. I was sure that it was Nesta who had brought Steve down and I'm trying to get him sent off! I didn't realise it was Gattuso. I've got the wrong man. The Milan players were trying all the tricks and delaying the kick by arguing that it wasn't a penalty. I had the ball and Garcia came running over to take it off me, but I wasn't having it; "You're not taking it."

It had been agreed before the game that Xabi would be on them. He had never taken one in anger, but to be honest we didn't have a regular penalty taker. I gave the ball to him and then stood halfway in the Milan half and watched. It all happened so quickly. Dida saved it low to his right, but you didn't have time to be gutted, Xabi's knocked in the rebound and we're back level. Unbelievable.

I've got the DVD and the fans are so funny. When we equalised everyone is going mad and there's this one fella who is just so shocked. He's just staring out into space in a daze. That always makes me laugh.

I didn't sprint over to Xabi; again I just got back into position. I was ecstatic but I needed a breather because I realised this was about to get tougher. At 3-2 it was all adrenaline and you're hungry. At 3-3 I'm thinking, "We'd better watch ourselves here." That's when the fear arrived on our side of the fence. Now we've got back in it you dread throwing away all that hard work. Riise had a shot a couple of minutes later, but then Milan emerged from their daze, got themselves sorted out and started to get their game together.

As time ticked on Jerzy came for a cross and missed it and was lucky that Djimi was on hand to block the shot on the line. Again, I had to scream at Jerzy. We were so close and you don't want to lose to a stupid goal. If Kaka dribbles through five players and scores a brilliant goal then fair enough, but let's not lose this to a soft goal. We've worked too hard.

Ancelotti brought on Jon Dahl Tomasson for Crespo and I was well pleased. Tomasson likes to drop deeper and it meant life was a little easier for us. Crespo was very difficult to play against as he makes such intelligent runs and has a tremendous burst of speed over the first few yards and the best way to play him was to have the ball ourselves. Simple. That's what we did second half.

It was Xabi Alonso's form that allowed us to do that. His passing is as good as anyone in Europe. They had Pirlo doing the same in the first half, but Xabi in that second period was just as brilliant. His ability to keep the ball meant we had so much more possession and when we had it Milan couldn't hurt us. I was fortunate to have played in the reserves with Jan Molby when I was a lad. Xabi isn't quite at Jan's level yet as a passer of the ball, but he's not far off. He can use both feet and knocks it long and short to great effect.

IT WAS ADRENALINE keeping us going. Milan had upped their game and we were tiring. Those incredible six minutes had taken it out of us, both physically, and, more importantly, emotionally. That kind of euphoria can be draining and we were hanging on with less than ten minutes to go. Fatigue was always going to come into this game and I found myself lunging in for tackles where I might have stayed on my feet. I was booked for a tackle on Shevchenko and got an evil glare from the Ukrainian as we jogged back. Oh well!

Ancelotti brought on Serginho. We had to bring Steve in at right-back to cope with him because we felt Vlad might struggle. That change made us a little bit more defensive and slowly you realised that we could only hang on for extra time and then penalties.

In injury time I played a poor cross-field pass that handed them possession. From that they broke into our box and had a man over. I had sprinted back thinking, "Please don't score from my cock-up", and found myself in the box facing their forward who was free out by the byline. I knew the fella couldn't score from the angle he had and so there was no point me closing him down because he would have just pulled it back to Shevchenko. I read what he had to do and managed to block Shevchenko's shot and we won a goal kick. That's my job. Block things, tackle. Strikers have to score goals and we defenders have to stop them. To me a last-ditch tackle or a clean sheet is like a goal.

These were tense moments. In the last minute Jaap Stam had a header that was going wide, but Kaka only had to touch it and it was in. He missed. It was so reminiscent of Gudjohnsen's miss in the semi-final. Things like that happen so quickly that you can't react, but if you look at Vlad's response on the line with his face in his hands you can see that our nerves were well frayed.

IT WAS TO be extra time and, as knackered as we all were, we were just ecstatic about being in with a shout. Cissé had come on by then and Rafa just told us to play deep and compact. He hoped that the Milan defenders had tired and he wanted Cissé to try and hit them on the break. That was the plan, but I think he had one eye on penalties.

I was having treatment for cramp and focusing on the most important thirty minutes of my career, but as I lay there I was taken by the fans who were still giving it their all. They had played such a massive part in not only the final but over our entire run to get there. Olympiakos, Juventus, the Chelsea games. They had been incredible. The contrast alone between the two semis was unbelievable. Stamford Bridge was so quiet compared to Anfield and I know that all players say their fans are the best, but ours have proven it time and time again. I also know that they support a team who are successful so they get to sing at finals and in Europe, but look how they travel abroad with all the banners and all the songs. They are world famous now I reckon.

The first half of extra time was very tight. Tomasson had one chance but Djimi did enough to put him off. The second period was all about us holding on. I stretched to stop a Serginho cross and my groin and my calves tightened with cramp. I was splayed out on the turf in pain. According to one TV pundit, who shall remain nameless, I had cramp in both groins! Our physio is being all nice and polite and waiting to be invited on to the pitch by the ref and I'm swearing. "Fucking get on, forget the fucking ref."

Rafa came over and thought I'd pulled my groin. We'd used all our subs, but I knew it was just cramp. I needed ten or 20 seconds without running and then went straight back on. The problem was, straight away another ball was whipped in and I've had to throw myself at it again. My legs were in bits.

There was no time to worry about that, though, as Sami and I were the busiest men there. In a way we were relishing it. As I say, it's your job and by the end we were both winning every header and getting first to every ball. Cramp or no cramp. It was the same against Juventus; out there in Turin we both were very comfortable despite the barrage they threw at us and in a perverse way you actually enjoy it.

In the last moments, though, Shevchenko had a header that we could do nothing about. He knocked it goalwards and from there it's slow motion again, you're just waiting for the net to bulge and to this day I can't believe he's missed it. Credit to Jerzy, he pulled off one amazing save and then followed up with another block, but it's a bad miss. I couldn't believe that once again we were still in the game and I just grabbed Jerzy and told him I loved him. I meant it too.

THAT WAS THE end. It was penalties. The manager came to us all and asked who wanted to take one. I said I did and just thought I'd be having one. Then he read out the list and I wasn't on it. We didn't come up with a five beforehand because you don't know how people are going to feel afterwards. I thought Garcia would have one for example. He was always scoring them in training, but the manager thought he was too tired. In fact, all the subs took one, so the manager clearly felt it was best for the fresher legs to have them.

Before we got going I ran over to Jerzy and gave him the pep-talk. I don't care what you call it, cheating, gamesmanship, I just wanted to win the European Cup and I told him to do his best to put them off. Jerzy is a dead nice fella, probably too nice and I knew he'd be dead courteous to them and shake their hands and all that. I said, "Don't worry about them. You don't know them, do you? Put them off lad."

It worked. Jerzy's giving it the Grobbelaar and they've missed their first two penalties and we've scored ours. When Cissé made it 2-0 you're starting to allow yourself to think "We might win this". That was the first time I really did that.

Then it all changed again.

Tomasson made it 2-1 and John Arne Riise was up next for us. Riise's was a great pen, beautifully placed, but it was another great save. Dida blocked it. Because it's John, we all expected him to blast it, he's got a bit of a shot on him you know, but he's placed it and it hasn't gone in.

That let them back in and Kaka made it 2-2, so Vlad's penalty was vital. If he scored his, we really had a great chance. He knocked it in and went mad. He was celebrating like we'd won and I was telling him to come back and calm down. I didn't want him to get carried away because it can come back to haunt you. All their players are watching him and I just thought this could get embarrassing. I remembered the Munich players getting a bit cocky in 1999 and then United came back to win, so you have to be careful.

They *had* to score their next penalty. I was standing next to Stevie and we see it's Shevchenko coming up to take it. There's no way *he's* missing, surely. Steve was up next for us, so I was saying to him, "Come on lad, you can win this for us." You don't expect the likes of Shevchenko to miss, but to be honest it was one of the worst penalties I've ever seen. It looks like he's trying to dink it, but it was nothing really. Jerzy got a good hand to it.

Pandemonium.

Suddenly my cramp's gone and I was off. I ran towards Jerzy, but then changed my mind and just wanted to be with the fans. Somehow I found my friends and family. I didn't have a clue where they were in the ground; I just ran and ran and then stopped and was grabbed by the supporters in the stand. My mates had come to the front. We did our celebrating and then, when I'd calmed down a but, I went over and shook the Milan guys hands. Stam came over and said, "Well done." They have to take some credit because they took it very well. I would have been suicidal.

TO SEE THAT trophy with our red ribbons around it was unbelievable. I have always watched foreign football and I never thought I'd be playing in a Champions League final. Halfway through the season we were losing at Southampton, Crystal Palace, Birmingham, and Burnley even. You don't even entertain ideas that you could be involved in a night like this.

UEFA's president Lennart Johansson actually made to give *me* the trophy. He thought I was the skipper! Some of those old UEFA guys haven't got a clue, I don't think. Steve had probably been rehearsing that moment since he was a kid and can you imagine if I had lifted it. There would have been hell to pay.

We took the cup around to our fans and it was just singing and dancing. Johnny Cash's Ring of Fire had become our theme tune and all of us were banging it out. That song had started on one of the coaches that my dad had been on. They would bring music for the away games and that was on this tape. They started singing it and it's taken off. They play it at Anfield now. It's become our theme tune. All the players had a CD with it on and it's still funny to see the Spanish guys all humming away to Johnny Cash.

After all that celebrating the dressing room was a bit of a come down. You're that tired there isn't much more you can do. It sounds strange doesn't it, but you are so drained that back in the dressing room we were just all sitting looking each other. There were some big grins mind you.

Gérard Houllier came in and chatted to us. I gave him one of my shirts. That was nice. Liverpool is a real family and it was good to see our ex-boss. He must have thought of what might have been.

We had a room at the top of our hotel where we had a big party. I couldn't really enjoy it because my phone was going off every two minutes with people wanting to get in. I kept having to go down to the fella on the door and lie, saying that this was my brother and could he come in. "You have very big family," he remarked. I do, but it's not that big!

We had the Cup with us and there were speeches, but we were all tired. The game had finished at about a quarter to one, so by three we were all knackered. Someone said that Milan Baros had dented the Cup, but I knew nothing about that. It's ours now, so it doesn't matter does it?

COMING HOME WAS amazing. The way we had won the game touched everyone and brought them out in their hundreds of thousands. On rooftops, hanging out of windows, standing on cars.

Everybody you meet has a story about what they did or how they felt at half-time. None more so than Evertonians. In a local pub in West Derby all the Everton fans were doing a conga at half-time. A few lads I know wouldn't go out and watch it because if we had won they would have been sick. At half-time they all phone each other and say, "Let's get our gear on and go to the pub for a good gloat." They've got their Everton tops on and made their way out and as they walk into the boozer it's 3-3. How gutted they must have felt?

Another fella, this time a Red, watched the first half and went to bed because he's up early for work. A couple of hours later he gets woken up by fireworks going off on the street and he's thinking, "What is happening here?" He gets up and turns the television on and there's Stevie Gerrard lifting the European Cup. Superb.

My medal sits proudly in the house. My dad has been taking it around the local schools for the kids to have photos taken with it. I still have to double take though when I see the words *LIVERPOOL, EUROPEAN CHAMPIONS*, but that's what that night made us and no one can take that away.

I got married just weeks after the final and had the trophy at my wedding. They allowed me to bring it along and we had it on the top table. What a guest-of-honour.

Leo Moynihan is a freelance sports writer. He has specialised in football and written on the beautiful game for a number of publications including FourFourTwo, The Sunday Telegraph, UEFA's Champions magazine. He has also covered a wide variety of other sports from Rugby Union to Curling. His first book, *Gordon Strachan, The Biography* was published in 2004 and was shortlisted for best new writer in the British Sports Book of the Year awards.